THE FUTURE LIES AHEAD OF US, BUT BEHIND US THERE IS ALSO A GREAT
ACCUMULATION OF HISTORY—A RESOURCE FOR IMAGINATION AND CREATIVITY.
I THINK WE CALL "CREATIVE" THAT DYNAMISM OF INTELLECTUAL CONCEPTION
THAT FLOWS BACK AND FORTH BETWEEN THE FUTURE AND THE PAST.

KENYA HARA
Designing Design
2007

CONTENTS

SECTION ONE: CREATING THE FIELD

THEORY AT WORK

G
D
T

REA

Edited by
Helen Armstrong

PRINCETON
NEW YORK

Published by
Princeton Architectural Press
37 East Seventh Street
New York, New York 10003

For a free catalog of books, call 1.800.722.6657.
Visit our website at www.papress.com.

This project was produced with editorial support from
the Center for Design Thinking, Maryland Institute College of Art.

Design Briefs Series Editor: Ellen Lupton

Special thanks to: Nettie Aljian, Sara Bader, Nicola Bednarek, Janet Behning,
Becca Casbon, Carina Cha, Penny (Yuen Pik) Chu, Russell Fernandez, Pete
Fitzpatrick, Wendy Fuller, Jan Haux, Aileen Kwun, Nancy Eklund Later, Linda
Lee, Aaron Lim, Laurie Manfra, John Myers, Katharine Myers, Lauren Nelson
Packard, Jennifer Thompson, Paul Wagner, Joseph Weston, and Deb Wood
of Princeton Architectural Press —Kevin C. Lippert, publisher

Library of Congress Cataloging-in-Publication Data
Graphic design theory: readings from the field / edited by Helen Armstrong.
    151 p. : ill. (some col.) ; 22 cm.—(Design briefs)
Includes bibliographical references and index.
ISBN 978-1-56898-772-9 (alk. paper)
1. Graphic arts. 2. Commercial art. I. Armstrong, Helen, 1971–
NC997.G673 2008
741.6—dc22
                                                    2008021063

SECTION TWO: BUILDING ON SUCCESS

THEORY AT WORK

SECTION THREE: MAPPING THE FUTURE

THEORY AT WORK

FOREWORD
WHY THEORY?

ELLEN LUPTON, DIRECTOR
GRAPHIC DESIGN MFA PROGRAM, MARYLAND INSTITUTE COLLEGE OF ART

This book is an introduction to graphic design theory. Each selection, written in its own time and place across a century of design evolution, explores the aesthetic and social purposes of design practice. All of these writers were—or are—visual producers active in the field, engaged with the realities of creating graphic communication. Why did they pause from making their work and building their careers to write about what they do? Why should a young designer today stop and read what they wrote?

Theory is all about the question "why?" The process of becoming a designer is focused largely on "how": how to use software, how to solve problems, how to organize information, how to get clients, how to work with printers, and so on. With so much to do, stopping to think about why we pursue these endeavors requires a momentary halt in the frenetic flight plan of professional development. Design programs around the world have recognized the need for such critical reflection, and countless designers and students are hungry for it. This book, carefully curated by emerging scholar and designer Helen Armstrong, is designed as a reader for history and theory courses as well as an approachable volume for general reading. Armstrong developed the book as graduate research in the Graphic Design MFA program at Maryland Institute College of Art, which has produced a series of collaboratively authored books. Hers is the first book from our program edited independently by a graduate student. Presented within its pages are passionate, intelligent texts created by people who helped build their field. These writers used their practical understanding of living processes and problems to raise philosophical, aesthetic, and political questions about design, and they used those questions, in turn, to inspire their own visual work as well as the work of people around them.

Design is a social activity. Rarely working alone or in private, designers respond to clients, audiences, publishers, institutions, and collaborators. While our work is exposed and highly visible, as individuals we often remain anonymous, our contribution to the texture of daily life existing below the threshold of public recognition. In addition to adding to the common beat of social experience, designers have produced their own subculture, a global discourse that connects us across time and space as part of a shared endeavor, with our own heroes and our own narratives of discovery and revolution. Few members of the general public are aware, for example, of the intense waves of feeling triggered among designers by the typeface Helvetica, generation after generation, yet nearly anyone living in a literate, urbanized part of the world has seen this typeface or characters inspired by it. Design is visible everywhere, yet it is also invisible—unnoticed and unacknowledged.

Creating design theory is about building one's own community, constructing a social network that questions and illuminates everyday practice—making it visible. Many of the writers in this book are best known for their visual work; others are known primarily as critics or educators. But in each case, a living, active connection to practice informs these writers' ideas. Each text assembled here was created in order to inspire practice, moving designers to act and experiment with incisive principles in mind. El Lissitzky, whose posters, books, and exhibitions are among the most influential works of twentieth-century design, had a huge impact on his peers through his work as a publisher, writer, lecturer, and curator. In the mid-twentieth century, Josef Müller-Brockmann and Paul Rand connected design methodologies to the world of business, drawing on their own professional experiences. Wolfgang Weingart, Lorraine Wild, and Katherine McCoy have inspired generations of designers through their teaching as well as through their visual work. Kenya Hara has helped build a global consumer brand (MUJI) while stimulating invention and inquiry through his work as a writer and curator.

A different kind of design theory reader would have drawn ideas from outside the field—from cognitive psychology, for example, or from literary criticism, structural linguistics, or political philosophy. Designers have much to learn from those discourses as well, but this book is about learning from ourselves. Why theory? Designers read about design in order to stimulate growth and change in their own work. Critical writing also inspires new lines of questioning and opens up new theoretical directions. Such ideas draw people together around common questions. Designers entering the field today must master an astonishing range of technologies and prepare themselves for a career whose terms and demands will constantly change. There is more for a designer to "do" now than ever before. There is also more to read, more to think about, and many more opportunities to actively engage the discourse. This book lays the groundwork for plunging into that discourse and getting ready to take part.

ACKNOWLEDGMENTS

The idea for this book sprang from conversations I had with Ellen Lupton as I prepared to teach a course in graphic design theory at the Maryland Institute College of Art in Fall 2006. In her roles as director of MICA's Center for Design Thinking and MICA's Graphic Design MFA program, Ellen provided invaluable guidance throughout the project. The Center for Design Thinking works with MICA students and faculty to initiate publications and other research projects focused on design issues and practices.

As both a student and a teacher at MICA, I have profited from the sheer dynamism of its Graphic Design MFA program. Special thanks go to my classmates, as well as the program's associate director, Jennifer Cole Phillips. I also recognize my own students, who provided a strong sounding board, allowing me to vet each stage of this book within the classroom. Gratitude is due, as well, to readers of my introduction, particularly art historian T'ai Smith. Her contemporary art seminar helped contextualize issues of anonymity and collectivism so important to graphic design. And, finally, thanks to the research staff of MICA's Decker Library, particularly senior reference librarian Katherine Cowan.

Essential to this project, of course, are the many eminent designers who graciously contributed their work. Special recognition goes to Shelley Gruendler for sharing her expertise and photo archive of Beatrice Warde. At Princeton Architectural Press, thanks goes to my editor, Clare Jacobson, for her thoughtful comments and ongoing support of the project. I hope this collection will inspire graphic designers to continue creating such vital theoretical texts.

Finally, to my family. To my daughters, Tess and Vivian, who will create by my side for a lifetime to come. My mother, Sarah Armstrong, who made annual essay contests a high point of my childhood. My father, John Armstrong, whose deep resounding voice I still hear when I read a verse of poetry. And to my husband, Sean Krause, a talented writer and the love of my life, without whom none of this would have been possible.

INTRODUCTION
REVISITING THE AVANT-GARDE

The texts in this collection reveal ideas key to the evolution of graphic design. Together, they tell the story of a discipline that continually moves between extremes—anonymity and authorship, the personal and the universal, social detachment and social engagement. Through such oppositions, designers position and reposition themselves in relation to the discourse of design and the broader society. Tracing such positioning clarifies the radically changing paradigm in which we now find ourselves. Technology is fundamentally altering our culture. But technology wrought radical change in the early 1900s as well. Key debates of the past are reemerging as crucial debates of the present. Authorship, universality, social responsibility—within these issues the future of graphic design lies.

COLLECTIVE AUTHORSHIP

Some graphic designers have recently invigorated their field by producing their own content, signing their work, and branding themselves as makers. Digital technology puts creation, production, and distribution into the hands of the designer, enabling such bold assertions of artistic presence. These acts of graphic authorship fit within a broader evolving model of collective authorship that is fundamentally changing the producer-consumer relationship.

Early models of graphic design were built on ideals of anonymity, not authorship. In the early 1900s avant-garde artists like El Lissitzky, Aleksandr Rodchenko, Herbert Bayer, and László Moholy-Nagy viewed the authored work of the old art world as shamefully elitist and ego driven. In their minds, such bourgeois, subjective visions corrupted society. They looked instead to a future of form inspired by the machine—functional, minimal, ordered, rational. As graphic design took shape as a profession, the ideal of objectivity replaced that of subjectivity. Neutrality replaced emotion. The avant-garde effaced the artist/designer through the quest for impartial communication.

After I I ʌSwiss graphic designers further extracted ideals of objectivity and neutrality from the revolutionary roots of the avant-garde. Designers like Max Bill, Emil Ruder, Josef Müller-Brockmann, and Karl Gerstner converted these ideals into rational, systematic approaches that centered on the grid. Thus proponents of the International Style subjugated personal perspective

1 Josef Müller-Brockmann, *The Graphic Artist and His Design Problems* (Zurich: Niggli, 1968), 7.

2 Michael Rock, "The Designer as Author," *Eye* 5, no. 20 (Spring 1996): 44–53.

3 The DIY (Do It Yourself) movement encourages people to produce things themselves rather than depend on mass-produced goods and the corporations that make them. New technologies have empowered such individuals to become producers rather than just consumers. For an explanation of the Free Culture movement, see http://freeculture.org. This movement seeks to develop a culture in which "all members are free to participate in its transmission and evolution, without artificial limits on who can participate or in what way."

4 For a discussion of the network structure and our society, see Pierre Lévy, *Cyberculture,* trans. Robert Bononno (Minneapolis: University of Minnesota Press, 2001).

5 Dmitri Siegel, "Designing Our Own Graves," Design Observer blog, http://www.designobserver.com/archives/015582.html (accessed April 28, 2008).

to "clarity" of communication, submitting the graphic designer to their programmatic design system. Müller-Brockmann asserted, "The withdrawal of the personality of the designer behind the idea, the themes, the enterprise, or the product is what the best minds are all striving to achieve."[1] Swiss-style design solidified the anonymous working space of the designer inside a frame of objectivity, the structure of which had been erected by the avant-garde.

Today some graphic designers continue to champion ideals of neutrality and objectivity that were essential to the early formation of their field. Such designers see the client's message as the central component of their work. They strive to communicate this message clearly, although now their post-postmodern eyes are open to the impossibility of neutrality and objectivity.

In contrast to the predominate modern concept of the designer as neutral transmitter of information, many designers are now producing their own content, typically for both critical and entrepreneurial purposes. This assertion of artistic presence is an alluring area of practice. Such work includes theoretical texts, self-published books and magazines, and other consumer products. In 1996 Michael Rock's essay "The Designer as Author" critiqued the graphic authorship model and became a touchstone for continuing debates.[2] The controversial idea of graphic authorship, although still not a dominant professional or economic paradigm for designers, has seized our imagination and permeates discussions of the future of design. And, as an empowering model for practice, it leads the curriculum of many graphic design graduate programs.

Out of this recent push toward authorship, new collective voices hearkening back to the avant-garde are emerging. As a result of technology, content generation by individuals has never been easier. (Consider the popularity of the DIY and the "Free Culture" movements.)[3] As more and more designers, along with the rest of the general population, become initiators and producers of content, a leveling is occurring. A new kind of collective voice, more anonymous than individual, is beginning to emerge. This collective creative voice reflects a culture that has as its central paradigm the decentered power structure of the network and that promotes a more open sharing of ideas, tools, and intellectual property.[4]

Whether this leveling of voices is a positive or negative phenomenon for graphic designers is under debate. Dmitri Siegel's recent blog entry on Design Observer, included in this collection, raises serious questions about where designers fall within this new paradigm of what he terms "prosumerism—simultaneous production and consumption."[5] Siegel asks, "What services and expertise do designers have to offer in a prosumer market?" The answer is, of course, still up for grabs, but the rapid increase in authorial voices and the leveling of this multiplicity of voices into a collective drive suggest the future of our working environment. Already designers increasingly create tools, templates, and resources for their clients and other users to implement. Graphic designers must take note and consciously position themselves within the prosumer culture or run the risk of being creatively sidelined by it.

UNIVERSAL SYSTEMS OF CONNECTION

At the same time that technology is empowering a new collectivity, it is also redefining universality. To understand how this crucial design concept is evolving, we need to take a look at how it initially emerged.

Members of the influential Bauhaus school, founded in Weimar in 1919, sought a purifying objective vision. Here, under the influence of constructivism, futurism, and De Stijl, a depersonalized machine aesthetic clashed with the subjective bent of expressionism, ultimately becoming the predominant model for the school. Artists like Moholy-Nagy equated objectivity with truth and clarity. To express this truth artists had to detach emotionally from their work in favor of a more rational and universal approach.[6]

Objective detachment spurred on other Bauhaus teachers, including Herbert Bayer and Josef Albers, who sought to uncover ideal forms for communicating clearly and precisely, cleansing visual language of subjectivity and ambiguity.[7] As Moholy-Nagy optimistically claims in his essay "Typophoto," in this new universal visual world, "the hygiene of the optical, the health of the visible is slowly filtering through."[8] In the 1970s and 1980s, postmodernism challenged the notion of universality by asserting the endless diversity of individuals and communities and the constantly changing meaning of visual forms.

The technology through which designers today create and communicate has quietly thrust universality back into the foundation of our work. Designers currently create through a series of restrictive protocols. Software applications mold individual creative quirks into standardized tools and palettes. The resulting aesthetic transformation, as Lev Manovich explores in his essay "Import/Export," is monumental.[9] Specific techniques, artistic languages, and vocabularies previously isolated within individual professions are being "imported" and "exported" across software applications and professions to create shared "metamedia." Powered by technology, universality has

6 For a more complete discussion of Moholy-Nagy at the Bauhaus, see Victor Margolin, *The Struggle for Utopia: Rodchenko, Lissitzky, Moholy-Nagy, 1917-1946* (Chicago: University of Chicago Press, 1997).

7 For a more complete discussion of the Bauhaus quest for visual language, see Ellen Lupton and J. Abbott Miller, eds., *The ABC's of Triangle Square Circle: The Bauhaus and Design Theory* (New York: Princeton Architectural Press, 2000), 22.

8 László Moholy-Nagy, "Typophoto," in *Painting, Photography, Film*, trans. Janet Seligman (Cambridge: MIT Press, 1973), 38-40.

9 Lev Manovich, "Import/Export, or Design Workflow and Contemporary Aesthetics," http://www.manovich.net (accessed April 28, 2008).

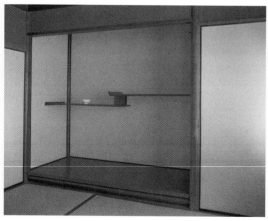

Anonimity v. authorship
Personal v. universal
Social detachment v. social
        engagement.

"Technology is fundamentally
altering our culture. But tech
wrought radical change in
early 1900's as well"

KENYA HARA MUJI advertisement, 2005 tea house posters. Hara's advertising philosophy for MUJI reinterprets old concepts of anonymity and universality. As he explains, "Communication becomes effective only when an advertisement is offered as an empty vessel and viewers freely deposit into it their ideas and wishes."[1]

1 Kenya Hara, *Designing Design*, trans. Maggie Kinser Hohle and Yukiko Naito (Baden: Lars Müller, 2007), 243.

moved far from the restrictive models of the past toward this new common language of, in Manovich's words, "hybridity" and "remixability" unlike anything that has come before.

This revamped hybrid universal language crosses boundaries between disciplines and individuals, between countries and cultures. In their essay "Univers Strikes Back," Ellen and Julia Lupton note it is "a visual language enmeshed in a technologically evolving communications environment stretched and tested by an unprecedented range of people."[10] Both global and local, the mass of work emerging from this universality and the resulting blurring of singular vision would boggle the minds of even the avant-garde. The universal systems of connection emerging today are different from the totalizing universality of the avant-garde, which sought to create a single, utopian visual language that could unite human culture. Today, countless designers and producers, named and unnamed, at work both inside and outside the profession, are contributing to a vast new visual commons, often using shared tools and technologies. Through this new "commonality" the paradigm of design is shifting.

SOCIAL RESPONSIBILITY

The same digital technology that empowers a collective authorship and enables a new kind of universal language is also inspiring a sharpened critical voice within the design community. Designers are actively engaging their societies politically and culturally, increasingly thinking globally inside a tightly networked world. As more and more designers, enabled by technology, produce both form and content, issues like sustainability and social justice are moving to the forefront. Designers are looking beyond successful business and aesthetic practices to the broader effects of the culture they help create.

Although currently recontextualized within the digital world, design-driven cultural critique, like issues of authorship and universality, is rooted in the avant-garde. Rodchenko, Lissitzky, Moholy-Nagy, and Bayer attempted to actively reshape their societies through design, pruning the chaos of life into orderly, rational forms. Both their language and their designs, included in this collection, portray the power of their societal visions. Beginning in the 1920s, Russian constructivists like Rodchenko and Lissitzky, in particular, helped enact a revolutionary avant-garde agenda. In the new Soviet Union, they transformed individual artistic intent into a collective utopian vision, hoping to achieve a better, more just, more egalitarian society. The fine artist became the unnamed worker, the "constructor."

10 Lupton, Ellen and Julia, "Univers Strikes Back," 2007. An edited form of this essay was published as "All Together Now," *Print* 61, no. 1 (January-February 2007): 28-30.

The detached neutrality of the International Style, particularly as practiced in the United States in the 1950s and 1960s, distanced designers from revolutionary social ideals. American designers like Paul Rand, Lester Beall, and Bauhaus immigrant Herbert Bayer used the almost scientific objectivity of Swiss design systems to position graphic design as a professional practice of value to corporate America. Rather than immerse their own identities within a critical avant-garde paradigm of social change, these designers sought to efface their identities in service to the total corporate image, bolstering the existing power structures of their day.[11]

In the late 1960s, the tide began to turn, leading to a renewed sense of social responsibility in the design community. A postmodern backlash against modernist neutrality broke out. Wolfgang Weingart, trained as a typesetter by typographic luminaries Emil Ruder and Max Bill and later a teacher at Basel Künstgewerbeschule, led a movement termed New Wave design in Switzerland.[12] He pushed intuition to the forefront, stretching and manipulating modernist forms and systems toward a more self-expressive, romantic approach.

In the United States Katherine McCoy, head of Cranbrook Academy of Art in Bloomfield Hills, Michigan, led her students from the 1970s to the early 1990s to engage more subjectively with their own work. While exploring poststructuralist theories of openness and instability of meaning, McCoy destabilized the concrete, rational design of the International Style. She emphasized the emotion, self-expression, and multiplicity of meaning that cannot be controlled within the client's message. And, in so doing, she shifted the user's gaze back to the individual designer, instating a sense of both voice and agency.

In the 1990s such rebellious forays into emotion and self-expression joined an increasing global awareness and a new concentration of production methods in designers' hands. Together, these forces motivated more and more graphic designers to critically reengage society. As the field shifted toward a more subjective design approach, a social responsibility movement emerged in the 1990s and 2000s.[13] Graphic designers joined media activists to revolt against the dangers of consumer culture. Kalle Lasn launched Adbusters, a Canadian magazine that co-opted the language and strategy of advertising. Naomi Klein wrote No Logo, an influential antiglobalization, antibranding treatise.[14] Thirty-three prominent graphic designers signed the "First Things First Manifesto 2000" protesting the dominance of the advertising industry over the design profession. Designers began generating content both inside and outside the designer-client relationship in the critique of society.[15]

11 For a discussion of avant-garde artists and corporate America, see Johanna Drucker, *The Visible Word: Experimental Typography and Modern Art, 1909-1923* (Chicago: University of Chicago Press, 1994).

12 New Wave design is also called New Typography, postmodernism, or late modernism.

13 For an overview of this social responsibility movement, see Steven Heller and Veronique Vienne, eds., *Citizen Designer: Perspectives on Design Responsibility* (New York: Allsworth Press, 2003).

14 Naomi Klein, *No Logo* (New York: Picador, 2002).

15 Rick Poynor, "First Things First Manifesto 2000," *AIGA Journal of Graphic Design* 17, no. 2 (1999): 6-7. Note: This manifesto references the "First Things First" 1964 manifesto authored by Ken Garland.

As the new millennium unfolds, graphic designers create within a vast pulsating network in which broad audiences are empowered to produce and critique. Within this highly connected world, designers like Kenya Hara, creative director of MUJI and managing director of the Nippon Design Center, develop innovative models for socially responsible design. For Hara, as for the avant-garde, the answer lies in the rational mind rather than individual desire. This new rational approach, however, incorporates a strong environmental ethos within a quest for business and design models that produce "global harmony and mutual benefit."[16] Issues of social responsibility, like graphic authorship, have also entered graphic design educational curriculum, encouraging students to look beyond formal concerns to the global impact of their work. No longer primarily led by restrictive modern ideals of neutral, objective communication, the design field has expanded to include more direct critical engagement with the surrounding world.

16 Kenya Hara, *Designing Design*, trans. Maggie Kinser Hohle and Yukiko Naito (Baden: Lars Müller, 2007), 429–431.

THE AVANT-GARDE OF THE NEW MILLENNIUM

This book is divided into three main sections: Creating the Field, Building on Success, and Mapping the Future. Creating the Field traces the evolution of graphic design during the early 1900s, including influential avant-garde ideas of futurism, constructivism, and the Bauhaus. Building on Success covers the mid to latter part of the twentieth century, looking at International Style, Pop, and postmodernism. Mapping the Future opens at the end of the twentieth century and explores current theoretical ideas in graphic design that are still unfolding.

Looking back across the history of design through the minds of these influential designers, one can identify pervasive themes like those discussed in this introduction. Issues like authorship, universality, and social responsibility, so key to avant-garde ideology, remain crucial to contemporary critical and theoretical discussions of the field.

Jessica Helfand, in her essay "Dematerialization of Screen Space," charges the present design community to become the new avant-garde. This collection was put together with that charge in mind. Helfand asks that we think beyond technical practicalities and begin really "shaping a new and unprecedented universe." Just as designers in the early twentieth century rose to the challenges of their societies, so can we take on the complexities of the rising millennium. Delving into theoretical discussions that engage both our past and our present is a good start.

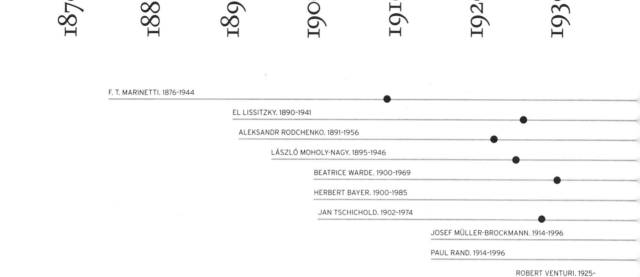

1870　1880　1890　1900　1910　1920　1930

F. T. MARINETTI. 1876-1944 ●

EL LISSITZKY. 1890-1941 ●

ALEKSANDR RODCHENKO. 1891-1956 ●

LÁSZLÓ MOHOLY-NAGY. 1895-1946 ●

BEATRICE WARDE. 1900-1969 ●

HERBERT BAYER. 1900-1985

JAN TSCHICHOLD. 1902-1974 ●

JOSEF MÜLLER-BROCKMANN. 1914-1996

PAUL RAND. 1914-1996

ROBERT VENTURI. 1925-

KARL GERSTNER. 1930-

JAN VAN TOORN. 1932-

TIMELINE

—— LIFESPAN OF EACH DESIGNER

● PUBLICATION DATE OF ANTHOLOGIZED TEXT

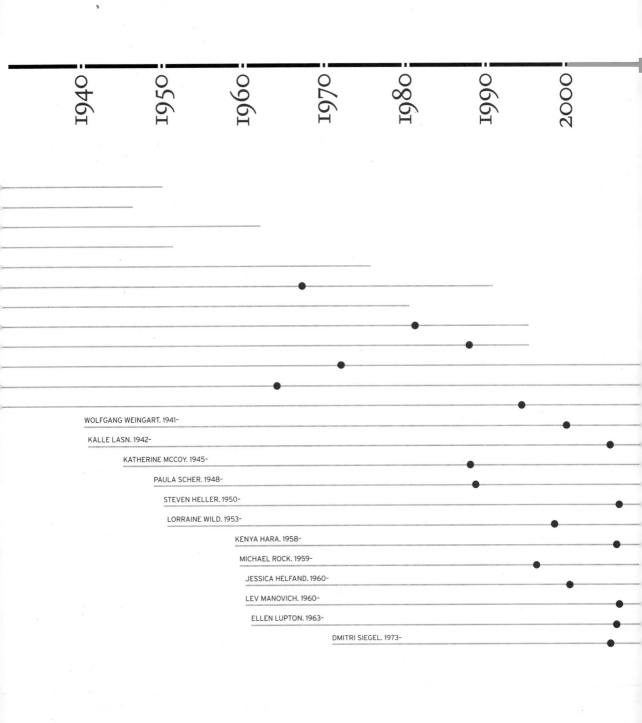

1940 1950 1960 1970 1980 1990 2000

WOLFGANG WEINGART. 1941–

KALLE LASN. 1942–

KATHERINE MCCOY. 1945–

PAULA SCHER. 1948–

STEVEN HELLER. 1950–

LORRAINE WILD. 1953–

KENYA HARA. 1958–

MICHAEL ROCK. 1959–

JESSICA HELFAND. 1960–

LEV MANOVICH. 1960–

ELLEN LUPTON. 1963–

DMITRI SIEGEL. 1973–

CREATING THE FIELD

AVANT-GARDE DESIGNERS HAD GUTS AND VISION. MOST WERE YOUNG PEOPLE, JUST IN THEIR TWENTIES. THEY WANTED NOTHING LESS THAN TO CHANGE THE WORLD. At the beginning of the twentieth century they unabashedly confronted their society through design. Surrounded by chaos—industrialization, technological upheaval, world war—they sought order and meaning. These artists spoke in manifestos and created posters, books, magazines, and typefaces using strikingly new visual vocabularies. They embraced mass communication; they abandoned easels. They treated the aesthetic conventions of symmetry and ornament like stale leftovers to be scourged at all costs. Instead the avant-garde looked to the machine for inspiration—sleek, functional, efficient, powerful. They tried to discover untainted visual forms that were fitting for the new modern world. Through such experiments they explored asymmetrical layout, activated white space, serial design, geometric typefaces, minimalism, hierarchy, functionalism, and universality. Out of their sweat, movements sprang up—futurism, Dadaism, De Stijl, constructivism, New Typography. Their ideas clashed and converged to form the modern foundation from which the graphic design industry emerged.

HERBERT BAYER Photomontage cover for the first issue of *bauhaus zeitschrift*, 1928. Bayer combines the tools of a graphic designer, basic geometric forms, and a page of type in his layout. Word and image come together to communicate to the reader.

F. T. MARINETTI BROKE THE SYMMETRICAL PAGE. HE CRACKED IT APART AND THEN PUT IT BACK TOGETHER USING BITS AND PIECES OF TYPE, PRINTERS' MARKS, AND ADS. First and foremost, he was a poet, but when in 1909 he published the "Manifesto of Futurism" in *Le Figaro*, a Paris newspaper, he embarked on a modern crusade that took him far beyond the realm of verse. In fact, it took him into the middle of a fledgling discipline called "graphic design." Marinetti was a showman, a scoundrel, and a fascist, but he matters today. Mainly out of economy and convenience, he used print to communicate with the masses—posters, books, flyers. He bent and twisted typography to better suit his poetry and his overall message of noise, speed, and aggression. In the end, the concrete, visual nature of type stood at the forefront of his work, exposed. He challenges us even now to embrace the future—in his words, to "exalt" in the "punch and the slap," to believe that entirely new forms are not only possible but imminent.

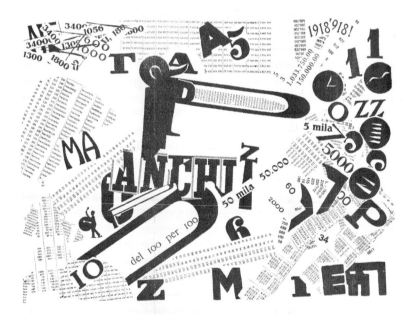

F. T. MARINETTI Foldout from
Les mots en liberté futuristes (The Futurist Words-In-Freedom), 1919.

MANIFESTO OF FUTURISM

F. T. MARINETTI | 1909

1. We intend to sing the love of danger, the habit of energy and fearlessness.

2. Courage, audacity, and revolt will be essential elements of our poetry.

3. Up to now literature has exalted a pensive immobility, ecstasy, and sleep. We intend to exalt aggressive action, a feverish insomnia, the racer's stride, the mortal leap, the punch and the slap.

4. We say that the world's magnificence has been enriched by a new beauty: the beauty of speed. A racing car whose hood is adorned with great pipes, like serpents of explosive breath—a roaring car that seems to ride on grapeshot—is more beautiful than the Victory of Samothrace.

5. We want to hymn the man at the wheel, who hurls the lance of his spirit across the Earth, along the circle of its orbit.

6. The poet must spend himself with ardor, splendor, and generosity, to swell the enthusiastic fervor of the primordial elements.

7. Except in struggle, there is no more beauty. No work without an aggressive character can be a masterpiece. Poetry must be conceived as a violent attack on unknown forces, to reduce and prostrate them before man.

8. We stand on the last promontory of the centuries!... Why should we look back, when what we want is to break down the mysterious doors of the Impossible? Time and Space died yesterday. We already live in the absolute, because we have created eternal, omnipresent speed.

9. We will glorify war—the world's only hygiene—militarism, patriotism, the destructive gesture of freedom-bringers, beautiful ideas worth dying for, and scorn for woman.

10. We will destroy the museums, libraries, academies of every kind, will fight moralism, feminism, every opportunistic or utilitarian cowardice.

11. We will sing of great crowds excited by work, by pleasure, and by riot; we will sing of the multicolored, polyphonic tides of revolution in the modern capitals; we will sing of the vibrant nightly fervor of arsenals and shipyards blazing with violent electric moons; greedy railway stations that devour smoke-plumed serpents; factories hung on clouds by the crooked lines of their smoke; bridges that stride the rivers like giant gymnasts, flashing in the sun with a glitter of knives; adventurous steamers that sniff the horizon; deep-chested locomotives whose wheels paw the tracks like the hooves of enormous steel horses bridled by tubing; and the sleek flight of planes whose propellers chatter in the wind like banners and seem to cheer like an enthusiastic crowd.

WHAT IS THERE TO SEE IN AN OLD PICTURE EXCEPT THE LABORIOUS CONTORTIONS OF AN ARTIST THROWING HIMSELF AGAINST THE BARRIERS THAT THWART HIS DESIRE TO EXPRESS HIS DREAM COMPLETELY?

F. T. MARINETTI
"The Founding
and Manifesto
of Futurism"
1909

ALEKSANDR RODCHENKO WAS THE SON OF A PROPMAN AND A LAUNDRESS. AT THE BEGINNING OF THE SOVIET REVOLUTION, HE TRANSFORMED HIMSELF FROM A PAINTER INTO SOMETHING ENTIRELY NEW. He became a constructor, an assembler, more engineer than artist. Inspired by Kazimir Malevich's *Black Square,* and the Suprematist movement as a whole, he turned away from representational art and grasped firmly to beliefs in utility and industry. Working intently in his self-designed leather workman's "production suit," Rodchenko utilized new technology and mass production in an attempt to give form not just to revolutionary concepts of functionalism and economy but to ideal Soviet citizens as well.[1] He embraced, redefined, and elevated graphic design as an essential force in society. In his "laboratory" Rodchenko and his great collaborator, love, and wife, Varvara Stepanova, repositioned artists as agents of social change standing at the center of a brave new world. We know Rodchenko's work. His distinctive style of geometric letterforms, flat color, diagonal composition, angled photography, and striking photomontage helped give visual voice to constructivism. His manifesto reminds us of the vision for society, and the designers within it, that these familiar images represent.

1 For a detailed discussion of Rodchenko's belief in the ideal Soviet citizen, see Victor Margolin, *The Struggle for Utopia: Rodchenko, Lissitzky, Moholy-Nagy, 1917-1946* (Chicago: University of Chicago Press, 1998).

WHO WE ARE
MANIFESTO OF THE CONSTRUCTIVIST GROUP

ALEKSANDR RODCHENKO, VARVARA STEPANOVA, AND ALEKSEI GAN | C. 1922

We don't feel obliged to build Pennsylvania Stations, skyscrapers, Handley Page Tract houses, turbo-compressors, and so on.

We didn't create technology.

We didn't create man.

BUT WE,

Artists yesterday

CONSTRUCTORS today,

I. WE PROCESSED

the human being

2. WE ORGANIZE

technology

I. WE DISCOVERED

2. PROPAGATE

3. CLEAN OUT

4. MERGE

PREVIOUSLY—Engineers relaxed with art

NOW—Artists relax with technology

WHAT'S NEEDED—IS NO REST
Who saw A WALL....
Who saw JUST A PLANE—
EVERYONE...AND NO ONE
Someone who had actually seen came and simply SHOWED:
the square.
This means opening the eyes TO THE PLANE.
Who saw an ANGLE
Who saw an ARMATURE, SKETCH
EVERYONE...AND NO ONE.
Someone who had actually seen came and simply SHOWED:
A line
Who saw: an iron bridge
a dreadnought
a zeppelin
a helicopter
EVERYONE...AND NO ONE.
We Came—the first working group of CONSTRUCTIVISTS—
ALEKSEI GAN, RODCHENKO, STEPANOVA
...AND WE SIMPLY SAID: This is—today
Technology is—the mortal enemy of art.
TECHNOLOGY....
We—are your first fighting and punitive force.
We are also your last slave-workers.
We are not dreamers from art who build in the imagination:
Aeroradiostations
Elevators and
Flaming cities
WE—ARE THE BEGINNING
OUR WORK IS TODAY:
A mug
A floor brush
Boots
A catalog
And when one person in his laboratory set up
A square,
    His radio carried it to all and sundry, to those who needed it and those
who didn't need it, and soon on all the "ships of left art," sailing under red,

ALEKSANDR RODCHENKO
Sketch of "production clothing,"
1922.

WORK FOR LIFE AND NOT FOR PALACES, TEMPLES, CEMETERIES, AND MUSEUMS. WORK IN THE MIDST OF *EVERYONE, FOR EVERYONE,* AND *WITH EVERYONE.*

**ALEKSANDR
RODCHENKO
"Slogans"
1921**

black, and white flags…everything all over, throughout, everything was covered in squares.

And yesterday, when one person in his laboratory set up

A line, grid, and point

His radio carried it to all and sundry, to those who needed it and those who didn't need it, and soon, and especially on all the "ships of left art" with the new title "constructive," sailing under different flags…everything all over…everything throughout is being constructed of lines and grids.

OF COURSE, the square existed previously, the line and the grid existed previously.

What's the deal.

Well, it's simply—THEY WERE POINTED OUT.

THEY WERE ANNOUNCED.

The square—1915, the laboratory of MALEVICH

The line, grid, point—1919, the laboratory of RODCHENKO

BUT—after this

The first working group of CONSTRUCTIVISTS (ALEKSEI GAN, RODCHENKO, STEPANOVA)

announced:

THE COMMUNIST EXPRESSION OF MATERIAL CONSTRUCTIONS

and

IRRECONCILABLE WAR AGAINST ART.

Everything came to a point.

and "new" constructivists jumped on the bandwagon, wrote "constructive" poems, novels, paintings, and other such junk. Others, taken with our slogans, imagining themselves to be geniuses, designed elevators and radio posters, but they have forgotten that all attention should be concentrated on the experimental laboratories, which show us

NEW

elements

routes

things

experiments.

—THE DEMONSTRATION EXPERIMENTAL LABORATORY AND MATERIAL CONSTRUCTIONS' STATION OF THE FIRST WORKING GROUP OF CONSTRUCTIVISTS OF THE RSFSR.

EL LISSITZKY TIRELESSLY TRAVELED—AND CROSS-POLLINATED. THIS INTENSE RUSSIAN CONSTRUCTIVIST SPURRED THE ONSLAUGHT OF AVANT-GARDE IDEAS SPREADING ACROSS EUROPE AND THE UNITED STATES IN THE EARLY 1920S. Denied entrance as a Jew to the art academy in Saint Petersburg, he went to Germany at the age of nineteen to study architecture. There he worked so relentlessly that his wife, Sophie, later connected his endless hours huddled over a drafting table to the "bent back and constricted chest" of his long struggle with tuberculosis.[1] During subsequent trips to Berlin, Lissitzky rubbed elbows with the luminaries of his time: Kurt Schwitters, Hans Arp, Piet Mondrian, László Moholy-Nagy, and Theo Van Doesburg. He appears at every influential avant-garde turn: major exhibitions, lectures at the Bauhaus, guest editor of Schwitters's journal, *Merz*. His drive produced influential paintings, exhibition design, photography, and typography. In "Our Book," he explores the new material forms of book design in his own era while predicting the dematerialization of it in our own increasingly digital world.

1 See Sophie Lissitzky-Küppers, "Life and Letters," in *El Lissitzky: Life, Letters, Texts*, trans. Helene Aldwinckle and Mary Whittall (London: Thames and Hudson, 1968), 16.

OUR BOOK

EL LISSITZKY | 1926

Every invention in art is a single event in time, has no evolution. With the passage of time different variations of the same theme are composed around the invention, sometimes more sharpened, sometimes more flattened, but seldom is the original power attained. So it goes on 'til, after being performed over a long period, this work of art becomes so automatic-mechanical in its performance that the mind ceases to respond to the exhausted theme; then the time is ripe for a new invention. The so-called technical aspect is, however, inseparable from the so-called artistic aspect, and therefore we do not wish to dismiss close associations lightly, with a few catchwords. In any case, Gutenberg, the inventor of the system of printing from movable type, printed a few books by this method that stand as the highest achievement in book art. Then there follow a few centuries that produced no fundamental inventions in our field (up to the invention of photography). What we find, more or less, in the art of printing are masterly variations accompanied by technical improvement in the production of the instruments. The same thing happened with a second invention in the visual field—with photography. The moment we stop riding complacently on our high horse, we have to admit that the first daguerreotypes are not primitive rough-and-ready things but the highest achievements in the field of the photographic art. It is shortsighted to think that the machine alone, that is to say, the supplanting of manual processes by mechanical ones, is fundamental to the changing of the appearance and form of things. In the first place it is the consumer who determines the change by his requirements; I refer to the stratum of society that furnishes the "commission." Today it is not a narrow circle, a thin upper layer, but "All," the masses.

The idea that moves the masses today is called "materialism," but what precisely characterizes the present time is dematerialization. An example: correspondence grows, the number of letters increases, the amount of paper written on and material used up swells, then the telephone call relieves the strain. Then comes further growth of the communications network and increase in the volume of communications; then radio eases the burden. The amount of material used is decreasing, we are dematerializing, cumbersome masses of material are being supplanted by released energies. That is the sign of our time. What kind of conclusions can we draw from these observations, with reference to our field of activity?

I put forward the following analogies:

Inventions in the Field of Thought-Communication	Inventions in the Field of General Communication
Articulated speech	Upright walk
Writing	Wheel
Gutenberg's letterpress	Animal-drawn vehicle
?	Motor-car
?	Aeroplane

I submit these analogies in order to demonstrate that as long as the book is of necessity a handheld object, that is to say, not yet supplanted by sound recordings or talking pictures, we must wait from day to day for new fundamental inventions in the field of book production, so that here also we may reach the standard of the time.

Present indications are that this basic invention can be expected from the neighboring field of collotype. This process involves a machine that transfers the composed type-matter onto a film, and a printing machine that copies the negative onto sensitive paper. Thus the enormous weight of type and the bucket of ink disappear, and so here again we also have dematerialization. The most important aspect is that the production style for word and illustration is subject to one and the same process—to the collotype, to photography. Up to the present there has been no kind of representation as completely comprehensible to all people as photography. So we are faced with a book form in which representation is primary and the alphabet secondary.

We know two kinds of writing: a symbol for each idea = hieroglyph (in China today) and a symbol for each sound = letter. The progress of the letter in relation to the hieroglyph is relative. The hieroglyph is international: that is to say, if a Russian, a German, or an American impresses the symbols (pictures) of the ideas on his memory, he can read Chinese or Egyptian (silently), without acquiring a knowledge of the language, for language and writing are each patterns in themselves. This is an advantage that the letter book has lost. So I believe that the next book form will be plastic-representational.

We can say that

(1) the hieroglyph book is international (at least in its potentiality),

(2) the letter book is national, and

(3) the coming book will be a-national: for in order to understand it,
    one must at least learn.

Today we have two dimensions for the word. As a sound it is a function of time, and as a representation it is a function of space. The coming book must be both. In this way the automatism of the present-day book will be overcome; for a view of life that has come about automatically is no longer conceivable to our minds, and we are left suffocating in a vacuum. The energetic task that art must accomplish is to transmute the emptiness into space, that is, into something that our minds can grasp as an organized unity.

With changes in the language, in construction and style, the visual aspect of the book changes also. Before the war, European printed matter looked much the same in all countries. In America there was a new optimistic mentality, concerned with the day in hand, focused on immediate impressions, and this began to create a new form of printed matter. It was there that they first started to shift the emphasis and make the word be the illustration of the picture, instead of the other way round, as in Europe. Moreover, the highly developed technique of the process block made a particular contribution; and so photomontage was invented.

Postwar Europe, skeptical and bewildered, is cultivating a shrieking, bellowing language; one must hold one's own and keep up with everything. Words like "attraction" and "trick" are becoming the catchwords of the time. The appearance of the book is characterized by (1) fragmented type panel and (2) photomontage and typomontage.

All these facts are like an airplane. Before the war and our revolution it was carrying us along the runway to the take-off point. We are now becoming airborne, and our faith for the future is in the airplane—that is to say, in these facts.

THE PRIVATE PROPERTY ASPECT OF CREATIVITY MUST BE DESTROYED. ALL ARE CREATORS AND THERE IS NO REASON OF ANY SORT FOR THIS DIVISION INTO ARTIST AND NONARTIST.

EL LISSITZKY
"Suprematism in
World Reconstruction"
1920

THE PRINTED SHEET TRANSCENDS SPACE AND TIME.
THE PRINTED SHEET, THE INFINITY OF THE BOOK, MUST
BE TRANSCENDED. THE ELECTRO-LIBRARY.

EL LISSITZKY
Merz, No. 4
1923

The idea of the "simultaneous" book also originated in the prewar era and was realized after a fashion. I refer to a poem by Blaise Cendrars, typographically designed by Sonia Delaunay-Terk, which is on a folding strip of paper, 1.5 meters in length; so it was an experiment with a new book form for poetry. The lines of the poem are printed in colors, according to content, so that they go over from one color to another following the changes in meaning.

In England during the war, the Vortex Group published its work BLAST, large and elementary in presentation, set almost exclusively in block letters; today this has become the feature of all modern international printed matter. In Germany, the prospectus for the small Grosz portfolio *Neue Jugend*, produced in 1917, is an important document of the new typography.

With us in Russia the new movement began in 1908, and from its very first day linked painters and poets closely together; practically no book of poetry appeared that had not had the collaboration of a painter. The poems were written and illustrated with the lithographic crayon, or engraved in wood. The poets themselves typeset whole pages. Among those who worked in this way were the poets Khlebnikov, Kruchenykh, Mayakovsky, Asseyev, together with the painters Rozanova, Goncharova, Malevich, Popova, Burlyuk, etc. These were not numbered, deluxe copies; they were cheap, unbound, paperbacked books, which we must consider today, in spite of their urbanity, as popular art.

During the period of the Revolution a latent energy accumulated in our young generation of artists, which merely awaited the great mandate from the people for it to be released and deployed. It is the great masses, the semiliterate masses, who have become the audience. The Revolution in our country accomplished an enormous educational and propagandistic task. The traditional book was torn into separate pages, enlarged a hundredfold, colored for greater intensity, and brought into the street as a poster. By contrast with the American poster, created for people who will catch a momentary glimpse whilst speeding past in their automobiles, ours was meant for people who would stand quite close and read it over and make sense out of it. If today a number of posters were to be reproduced in the size of a manageable book, then arranged according to theme and bound, the result could be the most original book. Because of the need for speed and the great lack of possibilities for printing, the best work was mostly done by hand; it was standardized, concise in its text, and most suited to the simplest mechanical method of duplication. State laws were printed in the same way as folding picture books, army orders in the same way as paperbacked brochures.

At the end of the Civil War (1920) we were given the opportunity, using primitive mechanical means, of personally realizing our aims in the field of new book design. In Vitebsk we produced a work entitled *Unovis* in five copies, using typewriter, lithography, etching, and linocuts. I wrote in it: "Gutenberg's Bible was printed with letters only; but the Bible of our time cannot be just presented in letters alone. The book finds its channel to the brain through the eye, not through the ear; in this channel the waves rush through with much greater speed and pressure than in the acoustic channel. One can speak out only through the mouth, but the book's facilities for expression take many more forms."

With the start of the reconstruction period about 1922, book production also increases rapidly. Our best artists take up the problem of book design. At the beginning of 1922 we publish, with the poet Ilya Ehrenburg, the periodical *Veshch* (Object), which is printed in Berlin. Thanks to the high standard of German technology we succeed in realizing some of our book ideas. So the picture book *Of Two Squares*, which was completed in our creative period of 1920, is also printed, and also the Mayakovsky book, where the book form itself is given a functional shape in keeping with its specific purpose. In the same period our artists obtain the technical facilities for printing. The State Publishing House and other printing establishments publish books, which have since been seen and appreciated at several international exhibitions in Europe. Comrades Popova, Rodchenko, Klutsis, Syenkin, Stepanova, and Gan devote themselves to the book. Some of them (Gan and several others) work in the printing works itself, along with the compositor and the machine. The degree of respect for the actual art of printing, which is acquired by doing this, is shown by the fact that all the names of the compositors and feeders of any particular book are listed in it, on a special page. Thus in the printing works there comes to be a select number of workers who cultivate a very conscious relationship with their art.

Most artists make montages, that is to say, with photographs and the inscriptions belonging to them they piece together whole pages, which are then photographically reproduced for printing. In this way there develops a technique of simple effectiveness, which appears to be very easy to operate and for that reason can easily develop into dull routine, but which in powerful hands turns out to be the most successful method of achieving visual poetry.

At the very beginning we said that the expressive power of every invention in art is an isolated phenomenon and has no evolution. The invention of easel pictures produced great works of art, but their effectiveness has been lost.

The cinema and the illustrated weekly magazine have triumphed. We rejoice at the new media that technology has placed at our disposal. We know that being in close contact with worldwide events and keeping pace with the progress of social development, that with the perpetual sharpening of our optic nerve, with the mastery of plastic material, with construction of the plane and its space, with the force that keeps inventiveness at a boiling point, with all these new assets, we know that finally we shall give a new effectiveness to the book as a work of art.

Yet in this present day and age we still have no new shape for the book as a body; it continues to be a cover with a jacket, and a spine, and pages 1, 2, 3....We still have the same thing in the theater also. Up to now in our country, even the newest theatrical productions have been performed in the picture-frame style of theater, with the public accommodated in the stalls, in boxes, in the circles, all in front of the curtain. The stage, however, has been cleared of the painted scenery; the painted-in-perspective stage area has become extinct. In the same picture frame a three-dimensional physical space has been born, for the maximum development of the fourth dimension, living movement. This newborn theater explodes the old theater-building. Perhaps the new work in the inside of the book is not yet at the stage of exploding the traditional book form, but we should have learned by now to recognize the tendency.

Notwithstanding the crises that book production is suffering, in common with other areas of production, the book glacier is growing year by year. The book is becoming the most monumental work of art: no longer is it something caressed only by the delicate hands of a few bibliophiles; on the contrary, it is already being grasped by hundreds of thousands of poor people. This also explains the dominance, in our transition period, of the illustrated weekly magazine. Moreover, in our country a stream of children's picture books has appeared, to swell the inundation of illustrated periodicals. By reading, our children are already acquiring a new plastic language; they are growing up with a different relationship to the world and to space, to shape, and to color; they will surely also create another book. We, however, are satisfied if in our book the lyric and epic evolution of our times is given shape.

EL LISSITZKY Cover
for *Veshch (Object)*, 1922.

LÁSZLÓ MOHOLY-NAGY CAME TO THE BAUHAUS IN 1923 AT THE AGE OF TWENTY-EIGHT. HE FLUNG OPEN THE DOORS AND FILLED THE HALLS OF THIS FAMOUS ART SCHOOL WITH TALK OF TECHNOLOGY. This Hungarian constructivist's obsessive discussions and experiments with photographic images—the photogram, the photoplastic, and, most importantly for the essay below, the typophoto—foresaw the emerging role of technology in both the aesthetics and practice of graphic design. Moholy-Nagy believed in the objective, collective, purifying effect of the camera on meaning. The integration of word and photographic image, in his mind, was a powerful antidote for the slippery nature of text. Each time we merge image and text in our own layouts, we reference his typophoto. In his book *Painting, Photography, Film*, he redirects our gaze through the "impartial approach" of photography, showing us even now how to experience reality anew. Moholy-Nagy stayed at the Bauhaus until 1928, influencing larger movements like the New Typography. In 1937, he emigrated to the United States and founded the New Bauhaus in Chicago, later changed to the Institute of Design.

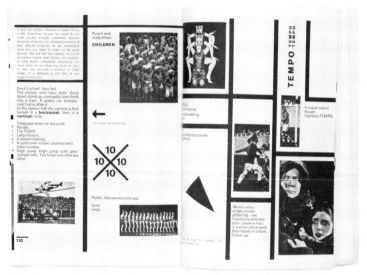

LÁSZLÓ MOHOLY-NAGY Spread
from *Malerei, Photographie, Film*
(*Painting, Photography, Film*), 1925.

TYPOPHOTO

LÁSZLÓ MOHOLY-NAGY | 1925

Neither curiosity nor economic considerations alone but a deep human interest in what happens in the world has brought about the enormous expansion of the news service: typography, the film, and the radio.

The creative work of the artist, the scientist's experiments, the calculations of the businessman or the present-day politician, all that moves, all that shapes, is bound up in the collectivity of interacting events. The individual's immediate action of the moment always has the effect of simultaneity in the long term. The technician has his machine at hand: satisfaction of the needs of the moment. But basically much more: he is the pioneer of the new social stratification, he paves the way for the future.

The printer's work, for example, to which we still pay too little attention, has just such a long-term effect: international understanding and its consequences.

The printer's work is part of the foundation on which the *new world* will be built. Concentrated work of organization is the spiritual result that brings all elements of human creativity into a synthesis: the play instinct, sympathy, inventions, economic necessities. One man invents printing with movable type, another photography, a third screen printing and stereotype, the next electrotype, phototype, the celluloid plate hardened by light. Men still kill one another, they have not yet understood how they live, why they live; politicians fail to observe that the earth is an entity, yet television (Telehor) has been invented: the "Far Seer"—tomorrow we shall be able to look into the heart of our fellow man, be everywhere and yet be alone; illustrated books, newspapers, magazines are printed—in millions. The unambiguousness of the real, the truth in the everyday situation, is there for all classes. The hygiene of the optical, the health of the visible is slowly filtering through.

What is typophoto? Typography is communication composed in type. Photography is the visual presentation of what can be optically apprehended. Typophoto is the visually most exact rendering of communication.

Every period has its own optical focus. Our age: that of the film; the electric sign, simultaneity of sensorially perceptible events. It has given us a new, progressively developing creative basis for typography, too. Gutenberg's typography, which has endured almost to our own day, moves exclusively in the linear dimension. The intervention of the photographic process has extended it to a new dimensionality, recognized today as total. The preliminary work in this field was done by the illustrated papers, posters, and by display printing.

"ART" COMES INTO BEING WHEN EXPRESSION IS AT ITS OPTIMUM, I.E., WHEN AT ITS HIGHEST INTENSITY IT IS ROOTED IN BIOLOGICAL LAW, PURPOSEFUL, UNAMBIGUOUS, PURE.

LÁSZLÓ MOHOLY-NAGY
Painting, Photography, Film
1925

Until recently typeface and typesetting rigidly preserved a technique that admittedly guaranteed the purity of the linear effect but ignored the new dimensions of life. Only quite recently has there been typographic work that uses the contrasts of typographic material (letters, signs, positive and negative values of the plane) in an attempt to establish a correspondence with modern life. These efforts have, however, done little to relax the inflexibility that has hitherto existed in typographic practice. An effective loosening up can be achieved only by the most sweeping and all-embracing use of the techniques of photography, zincography, the electrotype, etc. The flexibility and elasticity of these techniques bring with them a new reciprocity between economy and beauty. With the development of phototelegraphy, which enables reproductions and accurate illustrations to be made instantaneously, even philosophical works will presumably use the same means—though on a higher plane—as the present-day American magazines. The form of these new typographic works will, of course, be quite different typographically, optically, and synoptically from the linear typography of today.

Linear typography communicating ideas is merely a mediating makeshift link between the content of the communication and the person receiving it:

COMMUNICATION　　←　　TYPOGRAPHY　　→　　PERSON

Instead of using typography—as hitherto—merely as an objective means, the attempt is now being made to incorporate it and the potential effects of its subjective existence creatively into the contents.

The typographical materials themselves contain strongly optical tangibilities by means of which they can render the content of the communication in a directly visible—not only in an indirectly intellectual—fashion. Photography is highly effective when used as typographical material. It may appear as illustration beside the words, or in the form of "phototext" in place of words, as a precise form of representation so objective as to permit of no individual interpretation. The form, the rendering, is constructed out of the optical and associative relationships: into a visual, associative, conceptual, synthetic continuity: into the typophoto as an unambiguous rendering in an *optically valid* form.

The typophoto governs the new tempo of the new visual literature.

In the future every printing press will possess its own block-making plant, and it can be confidently stated that the future of typographic methods lies with the photomechanical processes. The invention of the photographic typesetting machine, the possibility of printing whole editions with X-ray radiography, the new cheap techniques of block making, etc., indicate the trend to which every typographer or typophotographer must adapt himself as soon as possible.

This mode of modern synoptic communication may be broadly pursued on another plane by means of the kinetic process, the film.

IN 1923 JAN TSCHICHOLD, A TWENTY-ONE-YEAR-OLD GERMAN TYPOGRAPHER, ATTENDED THE BAUHAUS EXHIBITION IN WEIMAR. HE WAS MESMERIZED. The exhibition was bursting with works of art and design influenced by De Stijl and constructivism. These vivid examples of the then emerging New Typography changed him. For the next decade Tschichold put aside his classical training, including his affection for symmetrical design, and became a powerful advocate of the new modern typographic movement. In 1928 he wrote his seminal book *The New Typography,* which opened these ideas to the printing industry in a clear, accessible manner. Theories became rules, while complex experiments became simple, reproducible systems. Tschichold's book remains essential to any typographic library. We remember him, though, not just for his passionate argument for the New Typography but also for his equally fervent turn against it. After being imprisoned by the Nazis and later escaping to Basel during World War II, Tschichold reconsidered. In the purifying order of the New Typography he sensed an element of fascism. During the latter part of his life he turned back to the classical typography of his early training.

THE NEW TYPOGRAPHY

JAN TSCHICHOLD | 1928

The essence of the New Typography is clarity. This puts it into deliberate opposition to the old typography whose aim was "beauty" and whose clarity did not attain the high level we require today. This utmost clarity is necessary today because of the manifold claims for our attention made by the extraordinary amount of print, which demands the greatest economy of expression. The gentle swing of the pendulum between ornamental type, the (superficially understood) "beautiful" appearance, and "adornment" by extraneous additions (ornaments) can never produce the pure form we demand today. Especially the feeble clinging to the bugbear of arranging type on a central axis results in the extreme inflexibility of contemporary typography.

In the old typography, the arrangement of individual units is subordinated to the principle of arranging everything on a central axis. In my historical introduction I have shown that this principle started in the Renaissance and has not yet been abandoned. Its superficiality becomes obvious when we look at Renaissance or baroque title pages. Main units are arbitrarily cut up: for example, logical order, which should be expressed by the use of different type sizes, is ruthlessly sacrificed to external form. Thus the principal line contains only three-quarters of the title, and the rest of the title, set several sizes smaller, appears in the next line. Such things admittedly do not often happen today, but the rigidity of central-axis setting hardly allows work to be carried out with the degree of logic we now demand. The central axis runs through the whole like an artificial, invisible backbone: its raison d'être is today as pretentious as the tall white collars of Victorian gentlemen. Even in good central-axis composition the contents are subordinated to "beautiful line arrangement." The whole is a "form" that is predetermined and therefore must be inorganic.

We believe it is wrong to arrange a text as if there were some focal point in the center of a line that would justify such an arrangement. Such points of course do not exist, because we read by starting at one side (Europeans for example read from left to right, the Chinese from top to bottom and right to left). Axial arrangements are illogical because the distance of the stressed, central parts from the beginning and end of the word sequences is not usually equal but constantly varies from line to line.

But not only the preconceived idea of axial arrangement but also all other preconceived ideas—like those of the pseudo-Constructivists—are diametrically opposed to the essence of the New Typography. Every piece of typography that originates in a preconceived idea of form, of whatever kind, is wrong. The New Typography is distinguished from the old by the fact that its first objective is to develop its visible form out of the functions of the text. It is essential to give pure and direct expression to the contents of whatever is printed; just as in the works of technology and nature, "form" must be created out of function. Only then can we achieve a typography that expresses the spirit of modern man. The function of printed text is communication, emphasis (word value), and the logical sequence of the contents.

left: Newspaper advertisement (Münchner Neueste Nachrichten) Bad, because: unnecessary ornaments, too many kinds of type and type sizes (7), centered design, which makes reading difficult and is unsightly.

right: The same advertisement, redesigned by Jan Tschichold. Good, because: no use of ornament, clear type, few sizes (in all, only 5 different types), good legibility, good appearance.

Captions and illustrations from *The New Typography* by Jan Tschichold.

Centered layout using lightweight sans serif has no visual effectiveness and reaches a "typographic low" for today (letterhead for a bookshop).

Caption and illustration from *The New Typography* by Jan Tschichold.

BUCHVERTRIEB
G   M   B   H

» DAS POLITISCHE BUCH «

BERLIN-SCHMARGENDORF

13.12.1926.
B.H./Sch.

THE METHOD OF NEW TYPOGRAPHY IS BASED ON A CLEAR REALIZATION OF PURPOSE AND THE BEST MEANS OF ACHIEVING IT. NO MODERN TYPOGRAPHY, BE IT EVER SO "BEAUTIFUL," IS "NEW" IF IT SACRIFICES PURPOSE TO FORM.

JAN TSCHICHOLD
"New Life in Print"
1930

Every part of a text relates to every other part by a definite, logical relationship of emphasis and value, predetermined by content. It is up to the typographer to express this relationship clearly and visibly through type sizes and weight, arrangement of lines, use of color, photography, etc. The typographer must take the greatest care to study how his work is read and ought to be read.

[…]

Working through a text according to these principles will usually result in a rhythm different from that of former symmetrical typography. Asymmetry is the rhythmic expression of functional design. In addition to being more logical, asymmetry has the advantage that its complete appearance is far more optically effective than symmetry.

Hence the predominance of asymmetry in the New Typography. Not least, the liveliness of asymmetry is also an expression of our own movement and that of modern life; it is a symbol of the changing forms of life in general when asymmetrical movement in typography takes the place of symmetrical repose. This movement must not, however, degenerate into unrest or chaos. A striving for order can, and must, also be expressed in asymmetrical form. It is the only way to make a better, more natural order possible, as opposed to symmetrical form, which does not draw its laws from within itself but from outside.

Furthermore, the principle of asymmetry gives unlimited scope for variation in the New Typography. It also expresses the diversity of modern life, unlike central-axis typography, which, apart from variations of typeface (the only exception), does not allow such variety.

While the New Typography allows much greater flexibility in design, it also encourages "standardization" in the construction of units, as in building.

An example of pseudo-modern typography. The compositor has the idea of a prefabricated foreign shape and forces the words into it. But typographic form must be organic, it must evolve from the nature of the text.

Caption and illustration from *The New Typography* by Jan Tschichold.

The old typography did the opposite: it recognized only one basic form, the central-axis arrangement, but allowed all possible and impossible construction elements (typefaces, ornaments, etc.).

The need for clarity in communication raises the question of how to achieve clear and unambiguous form.

Above all, a fresh and original intellectual approach is needed, avoiding all standard solutions. If we think clearly and approach each task with a fresh and determined mind, a good solution will usually result.

The most important requirement is to be objective. This, however, does not mean a way of design in which everything is omitted that used to be tacked on, as in the letterhead "Das politische Buch" shown here [see p. 37]. The type is certainly legible and there are no ornaments whatever. But this is not the kind of objectivity we are talking about. A better name for it would be "meagerness." Incidentally this letterhead also shows the hollowness of the old principles: without "ornamental" typefaces they do not work.

And yet, it is absolutely necessary to omit everything that is not needed. The old ideas of design must be discarded and new ideas developed. It is obvious that functional design means the abolition of the "ornamentation" that has reigned for centuries....

Today we see in a desire for ornament an ignorant tendency that our century must repress. When in earlier periods ornament was used, often in an extravagant degree, it only showed how little the essence of typography, which is communication, was understood.

AS A PUBLICIST FOR THE MONOTYPE CORPORATION, ONE OF THE LEADING TYPEFACE MANUFACTURERS, BEATRICE WARDE FILLED LECTURE HALLS FROM THE 1930S TO THE 1950S, SPEAKING TO PRINTERS, TYPESETTERS, TEACHERS, AND STUDENTS. QUITE LITERALLY, SHE BROUGHT ART TO THE MASSES. Through her prolific lectures and essays, she rose to meet the towering issue of the day—functionalism—with an approach based on tradition. In her mind, classical approaches to typography were not shackles to be cast aside but valuable history that should inform new work. During her long career at Monotype she worked with well-known typographer and historian Stanley Morison, who shared her passion for typographic history. She wrote many articles for the *Fleuron*, served as editor of the *Monotype Recorder,* and successfully launched the typeface Gill Sans to the British public. In October 1930 she gave an unforgiving lecture to the British Typographers Guild entitled "The Crystal Goblet, or Why Printing Should Be Invisible." Her lecture's metaphor of optimal typography as a window of glass, beautifully built yet transparent, is still relevant today, silencing the materiality of text while ushering forward a practical clarity of communication.[1]

1 For a detailed discussion of Warde, see Shelley Gruendler, "The Life and Work of Beatrice Warde" (PhD diss., University of Reading, 2003).

THE CRYSTAL GOBLET,
OR WHY PRINTING SHOULD BE INVISIBLE

BEATRICE WARDE | 1930

Imagine that you have before you a flagon of wine. You may choose your own favorite vintage for this imaginary demonstration, so that it be a deep shimmering crimson in color. You have two goblets before you. One is of solid gold, wrought in the most exquisite patterns. The other is of crystal-clear glass, thin as a bubble, and as transparent. Pour and drink; and according to your choice of goblet, I shall know whether or not you are a connoisseur of wine. For if you have no feelings about wine one way or the other, you will want the sensation of drinking the stuff out of a vessel that may have cost thousands of pounds; but if you are a member of that vanishing tribe, the amateurs of fine vintages, you will choose the crystal, because everything about it is calculated to *reveal* rather than to hide the beautiful thing that it was meant to *contain.*

Bear with me in this long-winded and fragrant metaphor; for you will find that almost all the virtues of the perfect wineglass have a parallel in typography. There is the long, thin stem that obviates fingerprints on the bowl. Why? Because no cloud must come between your eyes and the fiery heart of the liquid. Are not the margins on book pages similarly meant to obviate the necessity of fingering the type page? Again: the glass is colorless or at the most only faintly tinged in the bowl, because the connoisseur judges wine partly by its color and is impatient of anything that alters it. There are a thousand mannerisms in typography that are as impudent and arbitrary as putting port in tumblers of red or green glass! When a goblet has a base that looks too small for security, it does not matter how cleverly it is weighted; you feel nervous lest it should tip over. There are ways of setting lines of type that may work well enough, and yet keep the reader subconsciously worried by the fear of "doubling" lines, reading three words as one, and so forth.

Now the man who first chose glass instead of clay or metal to hold his wine was a "modernist" in the sense in which I am going to use that term. That is, the first thing he asked of this particular object was not "How should it look?" but "What must it do?" and to that extent all good typography is modernist.

Wine is so strange and potent a thing that it has been used in the central ritual of religion in one place and time, and attacked by a virago with a hatchet in another. There is only one thing in the world that is capable of stirring and altering men's minds to the same extent, and that is the coherent expression of thought. That is man's chief miracle, unique to man. There is no "explana-tion" whatever of the fact that I can make arbitrary sounds that will lead a total stranger to think my own thought. It is sheer magic that I should be able to hold a one-sided conversation by means of black marks on paper with an unknown person halfway across the world. Talking, broadcasting, writing, and printing are all quite literally forms of *thought transference*, and it is this ability and eagerness to transfer and receive the contents of the mind that is almost alone responsible for human civilization.

If you agree with this, you will agree with my one main idea, i.e., that the most important thing about printing is that it conveys thought, ideas, images, from one mind to other minds. This statement is what you might call the front door of the science of typography. Within lie hundreds of rooms; but unless you start by assuming that *printing is meant to convey specific and coherent ideas,* it is very easy to find yourself in the wrong house altogether.

Before asking what this statement leads to, let us see what it does not necessarily lead to. If books are printed in order to be read, we must distin-guish readability from what the optician would call legibility. A page set in 14-pt. Bold Sans is, according to the laboratory tests, more "legible" than one set in 11-pt. Baskerville. A public speaker is more "audible" in that sense when he bellows. But a good speaking voice is one that is inaudible as a voice.

BEATRICE WARDE
"The Crystal Goblet,
or Why Printing
Should Be Invisible"
1930

It is the transparent goblet again! I need not warn you that if you begin listening to the inflections and speaking rhythms of a voice from a platform, you are falling asleep. When you listen to a song in a language you do not understand, part of your mind actually does fall asleep, leaving your quite separate aesthetic sensibilities to enjoy themselves unimpeded by your reasoning faculties. The fine arts do that; but that is not the purpose of printing. Type well used is invisible as type, just as the perfect talking voice is the unnoticed vehicle for the transmission of words, ideas.

We may say, therefore, that printing may be delightful for many reasons, but that it is important, first and foremost, as a means of doing something. That is why it is mischievous to call any printed piece a work of art, especially fine art: because that would imply that its first purpose was to exist as an expression of beauty for its own sake and for the delectation of the senses. Calligraphy can almost be considered a fine art nowadays, because its primary economic and educational purpose has been taken away; but printing in English will not qualify as an art until the present English language no longer conveys ideas to future generations, and until printing itself hands its usefulness to some yet unimagined successor.

There is no end to the maze of practices in typography, and this idea of printing as a conveyor is, at least in the minds of all the great typographers with whom I have had the privilege of talking, the one clue that can guide you through the maze. Without this essential humility of mind, I have seen ardent designers go more hopelessly wrong, make more ludicrous mistakes out of an excessive enthusiasm, than I could have thought possible. And with this clue, this purposiveness in the back of your mind, it is possible to do the most unheard-of things, and find that they justify you triumphantly. It is not a waste of time to go to the simple fundamentals and reason from them. In the flurry of your individual problems, I think you will not mind spending half an hour on one broad and simple set of ideas involving abstract principles.

I once was talking to a man who designed a very pleasing advertising type that undoubtedly all of you have used. I said something about what artists think about a certain problem, and he replied with a beautiful gesture: "Ah, madam, we artists do not think—we feel!" That same day I quoted that remark to another designer of my acquaintance, and he, being less poetically inclined, murmured: "I'm not feeling very well today, I think!" He was right, he did think; he was the thinking sort; and that is why he is not so good a painter, and to my mind ten times better as a typographer and type designer than the man who instinctively avoided anything as coherent as a reason.

TYPE WELL USED IS INVISIBLE AS TYPE, JUST AS THE PERFECT TALKING VOICE IS THE UNNOTICED VEHICLE FOR THE TRANSMISSION OF WORDS, IDEAS.

BEATRICE WARDE
"The Crystal Goblet, or Why Printing Should Be Invisible"
1930

I always suspect the typographic enthusiast who takes a printed page from a book and frames it to hang on the wall, for I believe that in order to gratify a sensory delight he has mutilated something infinitely more important. I remember that T. M. Cleland, the famous American typographer, once showed me a very beautiful layout for a Cadillac booklet involving decorations in color. He did not have the actual text to work with in drawing up his specimen pages, so he had set the lines in Latin. This was not only for the reason that you will all think of, if you have seen the old typefoundries' famous *Quousque Tandem* copy (i.e., that Latin has few descenders and thus gives a remarkably even line). No, he told me that originally he had set up the dullest "wording" that he could find (I dare say it was from *Hansard*), and yet he discovered that the man to whom he submitted it would start reading and making comments on the text. I made some remark on the mentality of Boards of Directors, but Mr. Cleland said, "No: you're wrong; if the reader had not been practically forced to read—if he had not seen those words suddenly imbued with glamour and significance—then the layout would have been a failure. Setting it in Italian or Latin is only an easy way of saying 'This is not the text as it will appear.'"

Let me start my specific conclusions with book typography, because that contains all the fundamentals, and then go on to a few points about advertising. The book typographer has the job of erecting a window between the reader inside the room and that landscape that is the author's words. He may put up a stained-glass window of marvelous beauty, but a failure as a window; that is, he may use some rich superb type like text Gothic that is something to be looked at, not *through*. Or he may work in what I call "transparent" or "invisible" typography. I have a book at home, of which I have no visual recollection whatever as far as its typography goes; when I think of it, all I see is the Three Musketeers and their comrades swaggering up and down the streets of Paris. The third type of window is one in which the glass is broken into relatively small leaded panes; and this corresponds to what is called "fine printing" today, in that you are at least conscious that there is a window there, and that someone has enjoyed building it. That is not objectionable, because of a very important fact that has to do with the psychology of the subconscious mind. This is that the mental eye focuses *through* type and not *upon* it. The type that, through any arbitrary warping of design or excess of "color," gets in the way of the mental picture to be conveyed, is a bad type. Our subconsciousness is always afraid of blunders (which illogical setting, tight spacing, and too-wide unleaded lines can trick us into), of boredom, and of officiousness. The running headline that keeps shouting at us, the line that looks like one long word, the capitals jammed together without hair spaces—these mean subconscious squinting and loss of mental focus.

And if what I have said is true of book printing, even of the most exquisite limited editions, it is fifty times more obvious in advertising, where the one and only justification for the purchase of space is that you are conveying a message—that you are implanting a desire, straight into the mind of the reader. It is tragically easy to throw away half the reader-interest of an advertisement by setting the simple and compelling argument in a face that is uncomfortably alien to the classic reasonableness of the book face. Get attention as you will by your headline, and make any pretty type pictures you like if you are sure that the copy is useless as a means of selling goods; but if you are happy enough to have really good copy to work with, I beg you to remember that thousands of people pay hard-earned money for the privilege of reading quietly set book pages, and that only your wildest ingenuity can stop people from reading a really interesting text.

Printing demands a humility of mind, for the lack of which many of the fine arts are even now floundering in self-conscious and maudlin experiments. There is nothing simple or dull in achieving the transparent page. Vulgar ostentation is twice as easy as discipline. When you realize that ugly typography never effaces itself, you will be able to capture beauty as the wise men capture happiness by aiming at something else. The "stunt typographer" learns the fickleness of rich men who hate to read. Not for them are long breaths held over serif and kern, they will not appreciate your splitting of hair spaces. Nobody (save the other craftsmen) will appreciate half your skill. But you may spend endless years of happy experiment in devising that crystalline goblet that is worthy to hold the vintage of the human mind.

Beatrice Warde and Stanley Morison, c. 1935.

HERBERT BAYER HACKED AWAY ALL TRACES OF TYPOGRAPHY'S CALLIGRAPHIC PAST AS HE DREW HIS MODERN ALPHABET UNIVERSAL IN 1925. ARMED WITH A COMPASS, RULER, AND T SQUARE, HE REDUCED LETTERFORM DESIGN TO THE ESSENTIALS. Capital letters, eliminated; serifs, eliminated. As an instructor at the Bauhaus, he strove to revolutionize typography. His Universal alphabet was but one step in his lifelong quest to rethink the alphabet itself, reenvisioning it in new forms appropriate to machine-driven modern society. As exemplified by his work, Bayer urges us to go deep into the "underlying strata" of typography, moving beyond what he disdainfully describes as "trends of taste devoid of inner substance and structure, applied as cultural sugar-coating." In "On Typography" he highlights advances made in typography in the 1920s and looks to a radical new future, correctly foreseeing the widespread reshaping of typography imposed by new media. Exhibition designer, painter, architect, sculptor, photographer—Bayer managed to be immensely practical and rational while never losing the ideals he discovered at the beginning of his career.

ON TYPOGRAPHY

HERBERT BAYER | 1967

typography is a service art, not a fine art, however pure and elemental the discipline may be.

the graphic designer today seems to feel that the typographic means at his disposal have been exhausted. accelerated by the speed of our time, a wish for new excitement is in the air. "new styles" are hopefully expected to appear.

nothing is more constructive than to look the facts in the face. what are they? the fact that nothing new has developed in recent decades? the boredom of the dead end without signs for a renewal? or is it the realization that a forced change in search of a "new style" can only bring superficial gain?

it seems appropriate at this point to recall the essence of statements made by progressive typographers of the 1920s:

previously used largely as a medium for making language visible, typographic material was discovered to have distinctive optical properties of its own, pointing toward specifically typographic expression. typographers envisioned possibilities of deeper visual experiences from a new exploitation of the typographic material itself.

they called for clarity, conciseness, precision; for more articulation, contrast, tension in the color and black-and-white values of the typographic page.

HERBERT BAYER
"typography
and design at
the bauhaus"
1971

typography was for the first time seen not as an isolated discipline and technique, but in context with the ever-widening visual experiences that the picture symbol, photo, film, and television brought.

they recognized that in all human endeavors a technology had adjusted to man's demands; while no marked change or improvement had taken place in man's most profound invention, printing-writing, since gutenberg.

the manual skill and approach of the craftsman was seen to be inevitably replaced by mechanical techniques.

once more it became clear that typography is not self-expression within predetermined aesthetics, but that it is conditioned by the message it visualizes.

that typographic aesthetics were not stressed in these statements does not mean a lack of concern with them. but it appears that the searching went beyond surface effects into underlying strata. it is a fallacy to believe that styles can be created as easily and as often as fashions change. more is involved than trends of taste devoid of inner substance and structure, applied as cultural sugar-coating.

moreover, the typographic revolution was not an isolated event but went hand in hand with a new social, political consciousness and, consequently, with the building of new cultural foundations. the artist's acceptance of the machine as a tool for mass production has had its impression on aesthetic concepts. since then an age of science has come upon us, and the artist has been motivated more than ever to open his mind to the new forces that shape our lives.

new concepts will not grow on mere design variations of long-established forms such as the book. the aesthetic restraint that limits the development of the book must finally be overcome, and new ideas must logically be deduced from the function of typography and its carriers. although i realize how deeply anchored in tradition and how petrified the subject of writing and spelling is, a new typography will be bound to an alphabet that corresponds to the demands of an age of science. it must, unfortunately, be remembered that we live in a time of great ignorance and lack of concern with the alphabet, writing, and typography. with nostalgia we hear of times when literate people had knowledge, respect, and understanding of the subject. common man today has no opinion at all in such matters. it has come to a state where even the typesetter, the original typographer, as well as the printer, has lost this culture. responsibility has been shifted onto the shoulders of the designer almost exclusively.

in the united states the art of typography, book design, visual communication at large, in its many aspects, is being shelved as a minor art. it has no adequate place of recognition in our institutions of culture. the graphic designer is designated with the minimizing term "commercial" and is

HERBERT BAYER
"typography
and design at
the bauhaus"
1971

generally ignored as compared to the prominence accorded by the press to architecture and the "fine arts." visual communication has made revolutionary strides and real contributions to the contemporary world picture. yet, the artist-typographer represents a small number of typography producers compared to the output of the nation. their efforts must be valued as they keep the aesthetic standards from falling, and because they alone set the pace in taste.

there can be no doubt that our writing-printing-reading methods are antiquated and inefficient as compared to the perfection attained in other areas of human endeavor.

the history of our alphabet and any probing into its optical effectiveness expose a lack of principle and structure, precision and efficiency that should be evidenced in this important tool.

attempts have been made to design visually (to distinguish from aesthetically) improved alphabets. but redesigning will rest in just another typeface unless the design is primarily guided by optics as well as by a revision of spelling. this, in turn, reveals the need for a clearer relation of writing-printing to the spoken word, a reorganization of the alphabetic sound-symbols, the creation of new symbols. the type designer is not usually a language reformer, but a systematic approach will inevitably carry him to a point where he will ask for nothing less than a complete overhaul of communication with visual sound.

however unlikely the possibilities for the adoption of such far-reaching renovation appears at the moment, revitalization of typography will come:

a. from the increased demands made on the psychophysiologic
   apparatus of our perceptive senses;

b. from a new alphabet;

c. from the different physical forms that the carriers of typography will take.

the more we read, the less we see. constant exposure to visual materials has dulled our sense of seeing. overfed with reading as we are, the practice of reading must be activated. a new effort is needed to recapture and retain freshness. little known is the fact that the act of seeing is work, that it demands more than a quarter of the nervous energy the human body burns up. during waking hours your eyes almost never rest. in reading this article you must refocus as you skip from word to word. much energy is required for blinking and turning the eyeballs. more is needed by the tiny ciliary muscles to alter the shape of the crystalline lens for focusing. the effort of seeing contributes a large share to physical tiredness.

taking a closer look at present-day typographic customs, i make the following suggestions, believing that they offer immediate possibilities for both improvement and change.

[…]

UNIVERSAL COMMUNICATION

for a long time to come we will accept the existence of the different languages now in use. this will continue to pose barriers to communication, even after improved (possibly phonetic) writing methods have been adopted within all the languages. therefore, a more universal visual medium to bridge the gap between them must eventually evolve. first steps in this direction have, strangely enough, been made by the artist. now science must become a teammate and give him support with precise methods for a more purposeful handling of visual problems.

the book has been a standard form for a long time. a new spirit invaded the stagnant field of rigidity with the adoption of the dynamic page composition. an important extension was introduced with the recognition of supranational pictorial communication. with its combination of text and pictures, today's magazine already represents a new standard medium. while pictorial communication in a new sense has lived through a short but inspiring childhood, typography has hardly aspired to become an integrated element.

exploration of the potentialities of the book of true text-picture integration has only begun and will, by itself, become of utmost importance to universal understanding.

SQUARE SPAN

tradition requires that sentences follow each other in a horizontal continuous sequence. paragraphs are used to ease perception by a slight break. there is no reason for this to be the only method to transmit language to the eye. sentences could as well follow each other vertically or otherwise, if it would facilitate reading.

following is an excerpt of a letter from "the reporter of direct mail advertising": "square span" is putting words into thought groups of two or three short lines, such as

after a short time	you will begin thinking	in easily understood	groups of words
you will automatically stop	confusing your sentences	with complicated phrases	and unnecessary words

typewriters and typesetting machines would have to be adjusted to this method. text written in logical, short thought groups lends itself best. the advantages of grouping words support the theory that we do not read individual letters, but words or phrases. this poses a new challenge for the typographer.

text in color black printing on white stock, because of its extreme opposites, is not entirely satisfactory. the eye forms complementary images. flickering and optical illusions occur, however minimized they may be in a small typeface. they can be reduced if the contrast of black on white is softened by gray printing on white stock; black printing on gray, yellow, light blue, or light green stock; brown, dark green, or dark blue printing on light colored stock. the colors of printing in relation to the colors of stock need not necessarily be chosen for harmonies; it is the power of controlled contrast that must be retained.

CHANGE OF IMPACT

furthermore, a great easing of reading is effected and freshness of perception is prolonged if a book is made up with a sequence of pages of different colored stock printed in various colors. which color follows another is less important than that the hues be approximately of equal value to safeguard continuity. "square span" writing was developed by robert b. andrews, dallas, texas.

dr. w. h. bates has recommended a frequent shifting to aid in refocusing a fixed stare caused by the eye-tiring monotony of reading matter. the typographer can support this recommendation by the above change of impact through color.

NEW SLAVES

speculation into the future (perhaps not so distant) leads me to assume that methods of communication will change drastically.

the storage of books will be replaced by microfilms, which in turn will change the design of libraries. computing machines can already substitute for printed matter by storing knowledge. they will have any and all desired information available and ready when needed on short call, faster, more completely than research teams could, relieving and unburdening our brains of memory ballast. this suggests that we will write and read less and less, and the book may be eliminated altogether. the time may come when we have learned to communicate by electronic or extrasensory means....

formalism and the straightjacket of a style lead to a dead end. the self-changing pulse of life is the nature of things with its unlimited forms and ways of expression. this we must recognize and not make new clichés out of old formulas.

abcdefghi
jklmnopqr
stuvwxyz

HERBERT BAYER: Abb.1. Alfabet
„g" und „k" sind noch als
unfertig zu betrachten

Beispiel eines Zeichens
in größerem Maßstab
Präzise optische Wirkung

sturm blond

Abb. 2. Anwendung

HERBERT BAYER universal, a
geometric alphabet consisting only
of lowercase letters, designed by
Bayer at the Bauhaus, 1925.

F. T. MARINETTI Spread of *Parole in Libertà Futuriste, olfattive, tattili, termiche (The Words-in-freedom, Futurist, Olfactive, Tactilist, Thermal)*, 1932. This book is a high point of futurist experimental bookmaking. It was printed by a lithographic process in many colors on metal sheets. The layout is explosive, emphasizing the materiality of the work by simultaneously pushing forward and breaking apart the printer's metal grid.

F. T. MARINETTI FUTURISTA

ZANG

TUMB TUMB

ADRIANOPOLI   OTTOBRE 1912

TUUUMB IN LIBERTÀ

PAROLE

TUUUM TUUUM TUUUM

EDIZIONI FUTURISTE
DI "POESIA"
Corso Venezia, 61 - MILANO
1914

F. T. MARINETTI Cover for
Zang Tumb Tumb, 1914. In this book
Marinetti celebrates the Battle of
Tripoli through his concept of words-
in-freedom. According to this futurist
concept, typography should reflect
the raw, emotional power of language
rather than rely on established rules
of syntax and punctuation.

As Marinetti explained in his 1913
manifesto, "Destruction of Syntax—
Untrammeled Imagination—Words-in-
Freedom," "My revolution is directed
against the so-called typographic
harmony of the page, which contra-
dicts the ebb and flow, the leaps and
bounds of style that surge over the
page.... I don't want to evoke an idea
or a sensation with these traditionalist
charms or affectations, I want to seize
them roughly and hurl them straight
in the reader's face."[1]

1 F. T. Marinetti, "Destruction of Syntax—
Untrammeled Imagination—Words-in-Freedom,"
in *F. T. Marinetti: Critical Writings,* ed. Günter
Berghaus, trans. Doug Thompson (New York:
Farrar, Straus and Giroux, 2006), 128.

Constructivism

ALEKSANDR RODCHENKO
Ad for Lengiz, the Leningrad
section of the state publishing
house, Gosizdat, 1924. The text
reads "Books on Every Subject."
As a founding member of Russian
constructivism, Rodchenko cast
off representational art, assembling
instead a collective voice through
the abstract visual vocabulary
he established for the revolution.
As reflected in the ad above, this
language included bold planes
of flat color, asymmetric balance,
sans serif typefaces, and densely
filled space.

EL LISSITZKY Cover and
spread from *Dlia Golosa* (*For the
Voice,* or *Read Out Loud*), 1923.
Lissitzky collaborated with Russian
futurist poet Vladimir Mayakovsky
to produce this collection of
Mayakovsky's poetry.[1] Unlike his
compatriot Rodchenko, who often
had to handcraft his letterforms,
world-traveler Lissitzky was able
to harness the superior printing
expertise of Berlin in this book.
Lissitzky took full creative advantage of the use of letterpress
typography, forming innovative
abstract images through standard
typographic forms. To emphasize
the functionality of the piece, he
created a thumb index to guide
the reader.

1 For a discussion of *Dlia Golosa* and other
constructivist books, see Margit Rowell and
Deborah Wye, "Constructivist Book Design:
Shaping the Proletarian Conscience," in *The
Russian Avant-Garde Book: 1910-1934* (New
York: Museum of Modern Art, 2002), 50-59.

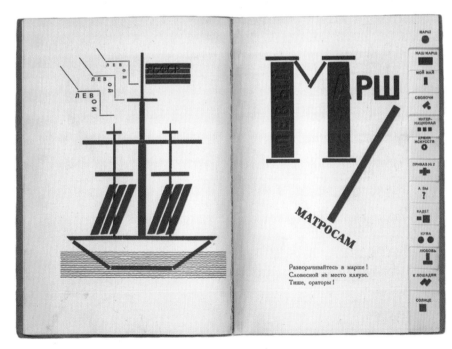

The Bauhaus and New Typography

HERBERT BAYER Bauhaus sixtieth-birthday exhibition poster for Wassily Kandinsky, 1926. Bauhaus teachers like Bayer attempted to replace personal artistic vision with abstract, neutral forms, a visual language accessible to all. Ironically, this same visual language has become a recognizable Bauhaus style. Bayer was the first Bauhaus professor of the typography and graphic design workshops and became the public face of its graphic design program.

HERBERT BAYER Poster for exhibition of European arts and crafts in Leipzig, 1927. In addition to his role as the Bauhaus typographic instructor, Bayer produced the bulk of the graphic design that represented the school to the public. In essence, his individual style became the Bauhaus Inc. style, as demonstrated in the familiar poster above.

JAN TSCHICHOLD Poster for the film *Napoleon*, 1927. A movement called the New Typography emerged from the Bauhaus search for a universal language and the resulting typographic experimentation. Tschichold codified this movement for the printing industry in his book *The New Typography* in 1928, which turned Bauhaus ideals into straightforward rules. Through such texts and designs, Tschichold attempted to establish norms for practicing typography and graphic design.

protégez l'enfant !

BUILDING ON SUCCESS

IN THE 1950S, 1960S, AND 1970S GRAPHIC DESIGN BECAME A PROFESSION. SWISS DESIGNERS LIKE JOSEF MÜLLER-BROCKMANN AND KARL GERSTNER TURNED REVOLUTIONARY AVANT-GARDE IDEALS INTO FORMAL METHOD-OLOGIES, DETACHING DESIGN FROM A DISRUPTIVE AESTHETIC AGENDA.

The resulting International Style leapt from Europe to the United States, spreading values of neutrality, objectivity, and rationality expressed through tightly gridded layouts and restricted typography. Business and design joined forces as iconic American designers Paul Rand and Bauhaus immigrant Herbert Bayer used Swiss approaches to construct powerful corporate identity systems. In the 1960s rebellion broke out. Wolfgang Weingart pioneered the New Wave of Swiss design. Legibility and clarity gave way to emotion and intuition. Modern turned to postmodern as the Pop movement took form. In America, Katherine McCoy led her Cranbrook students from the 1970s to 1990s into the heart of poststructuralism, turning design into complex discourse to be decoded by the reader. Powerful modern design tenets were shaken; designers lost faith in the rationality, objectivity, and universalism of the early century.

JOSEF MÜLLER-BROCKMANN
protégez l'enfant! Public awareness poster
for Swiss Automobile Club, 1953.

KARL GERSTNER CREATED A RATIONAL, SYSTEMATIC APPROACH TO GRAPHIC DESIGN. AS A BOY IN BASEL THIS PIONEER OF SWISS TYPOGRAPHY LONGED TO BE A CHEMIST. Unable to afford the extensive training, he turned instead to the visual synthesis of graphic design. Gerstner merged art with science. He developed a comprehensive system capable of generating a broad range of design solutions, and he connected this system to the evolving field of computer programming. Gerstner detailed his approach in *Designing Programmes,* a book that became a 1960s cult classic. For three decades he ran GGK, the advertising agency he founded with Markus Kutter in 1959. His early work with systems-oriented design reveals, in his words, "How much computers change—or can change—not only the procedure of the work but the work itself."[1] Gerstner's parallel career as a fine artist steeped in the Concrete Art movement consistently informed the precision of his commercial work.

1 Manfred Kröplien, "Status Quo at 66," in Karl Gerstner, *Review of 5 x 10 Years of Graphic Design etc.* (Ostfildern-Ruit, Germany: Hatje Cantz, 2001), 242.

DESIGNING PROGRAMMES

KARL GERSTNER | 1964

PROGRAMME AS LOGIC

Instead of solutions for problems, programmes for solutions—the subtitle can also be understood in these terms: for no problem (so to speak) is there an absolute solution. Reason: the possibilities cannot be delimited absolutely. There is always a group of solutions, one of which is the best under certain conditions.

To describe the problem is part of the solution. This implies: not to make creative decisions as prompted by feeling but by intellectual criteria. The more exact and complete these criteria are, the more creative the work becomes. The creative process is to be reduced to an act of selection. Designing means: to pick out determining elements and combine them. Seen in these terms, designing calls for method. The most suitable I know is the one Fritz Zwicky has developed, although actually his is intended for scientists rather than designers. (Die morphologische Forschung, 1953, Kommissionsverlag, Winterthur.) I have produced the diagram below in accordance with his instructions and, following his terminology, I have called it "the morphological box of the typogram." It contains the criteria—the parameters on the left, the relative components on the right—following which marks and signs are to be designed from letters.

The criteria are rough. As the work proceeds, of course, they are to be refined as desired. The components are to be made into parameters and new components are to be specified, etc. Moreover, they are not only rough, they are also not self-contained. The component "something else" is the parcel in which the leftovers are packed if the parameter does not break down neatly. The designations are imprecise in some cases. There are many imperfections. But it is precisely in drawing up the scheme, in striving for perfection, that the work really lies. The work is not diminished; it is merely transferred to another plane.

The inadequacy of this box is my own and not inherent in the method. Even so: it contains thousands of solutions that—as could be shown by checking an example—are arrived at by the blind concatenation of components. It is a kind of designing automatic.

I APPRECIATE THE MORAL IMPERATIVE THAT NO TASK IS SO INSIGNIFICANT THAT IT NEEDN'T BE ACCOMPLISHED IN KEEPING WITH THE HIGHEST STANDARD.

KARL GERSTNER
Review of 5 x 10 Years of Graphic Design etc.
2001

a   Basis

1. Components	11. Word	12. Abbreviation	13. Word group	14. Combined	
2. Typeface	21. Sans-serif	22. Roman	23. German	24. Some other	25. Combined
3. Technique	31. Written	32. Drawn	33. Composed	34. Some other	35. Combined

b   Colour

1. Shade	11. Light	12. Medium	13. Dark	14. Combined
2. Value	21. Chromatic	22. Achromatic	23. Mixed	24. Combined

c   Appearance

1. Size	11. Small	12. Medium	13. Large	14. Combined
2. Proportion	21. Narrow	22. Usual	23. Broad	24. Combined
3. Boldness	31. Lean	32. Normal	33. Fat	34. Combined
4. Inclination	41. Upright	42. Oblique	43. Combined	

d   Expression

1. Reading direction	11. From left to right	12. From top to bottom	13. From bottom to top	14. Otherwise	15. Combined
2. Spacing	21. Narrow	22. Normal	23. Wide	24. Combined	
3. Form	31. Unmodified	32. Mutilated	33. Projected	34. Something else	35. Combined
4. Design	41. Unmodified	42. Something omitted	43. Something replaced	44. Something added	45. Combined

SOLUTIONS FROM THE PROGRAMME

(Not all the solutions were found with the aid of the morphological box. But all those found can be assigned to a place in it and analyzed.)

If all the components contained in the trademark *intermöbel* are added, we obtain the following chain:

a 11. (word) - 21. (sans-serif) - 33. (composed)

b 14. (shades combined, viz. light and dark) -12. (achromatic)

c 12. (size immaterial, therefore medium) - 22. (proportion usual) - 33. (fat) - 41. (roman)

d 11. (from left to right) - 22. (normal spacing) - 31. (form unmodified) - 43. (something replaced, viz., the face of the letter r by superimposition of the two parts of the word).

Not all the components are of equal importance; only two are actually decisive: b 14 + d 43.

The importance of "combined" is shown in example b 14: the components light-medium-dark are not very expressive in themselves because they do not represent an assessable value (apart from black always being dark). But if letters of varying degrees of darkness are combined (as here) the parameter of shade may be the point at which the solution crystallizes out.

Parameters as points of crystallization: I will illustrate all those in the section "Expression" by the following examples:

"Reading direction" determines the expression of the typograms Krupp and National Zeitung. In both instances the component d 15 (combined) forms the basis. In Krupp d 11 (from left to right) is combined with d 14 (otherwise, i.e., from right to left).

In the case of National Zeitung the components are d 12 and 13.

"Spacing," once again combined in the component, is determining in Braun Electric and Autokredit A.G.

22

intermöbel

23

KЯUPP 1811
KRUPP 1961

24

National Zeitung

25

B r a u n Electric I n t e r n a t i o n a l SA

26

A U T O K R E D I T

PROGRAMME AS GRID

Is the grid a programme? Let me put it more specifically: if the grid is considered as a proportional regulator, a system, it is a programme par excellence. Squared paper is a (arithmetic) grid, but not a programme. Unlike, say, the (geometric) module of Le Corbusier, which can, of course, be used as a grid but is primarily a programme. Albert Einstein said of the module: "It is a scale of proportions that makes the bad difficult and the good easy." That is a programmatic statement of what I take to be the aim of "Designing Programmes."

The typographic grid is a proportional regulator for composition, tables, pictures, etc. It is a formal programme to accommodate x unknown items. The difficulty is: to find the balance, the maximum of conformity to a rule with the maximum of freedom. Or: the maximum of constants with the greatest possible variability.

In our agency we have evolved the "mobile grid." An example is the arrangement below: the grid for the periodical *Capital*.

The basic unit is 10 points; the size of the basic typeface including the lead. The text and picture area are divided at the same time into one, two, three, four, five, and six columns. There are 58 units along the whole width. This number is a logical one when there are always two units between the columns. That is: it divides in every case without a remainder: with two columns the 58 units are composed of 2 x 28 + 2 (space between columns); with 3 columns 3 x 18 + 2 x 2; with 4 columns 4 x 13 + 3 x 2; with 5 columns 5 x 10 + 4 x 2; with 6 columns 6 x 8 + 5 x 2 10-point units.

The grid looks complicated to anyone not knowing the key. For the initiate it is easy to use and (almost) inexhaustible as a programme.

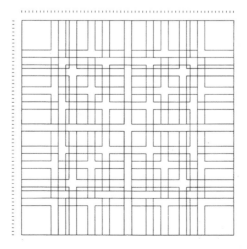

JOSEF MÜLLER-BROCKMANN DIVIDED AND ORDERED GRAPHIC DESIGN INTO THE GRID OF SWISS TYPOGRAPHY. HE TOOK DESIGN ELEMENTS THAT WERE SUBJECTIVE, IRRATIONAL, AND CHAOTIC AND BROUGHT THEM UNDER TIGHT, MEASURED CONTROL. He delved deep into form and content, spending his life in Zurich paring down his work to the essentials necessary for what he considered an objective—even timeless—method of communication. The grid was key to this pursuit. As Müller-Brockmann's notes in the essay at right, "Working within the grid system means submitting to laws of universal validity." He popularized the grid while spreading the principles of Swiss typography internationally through graphic design, lectures, and publications. In 1958 he founded *New Graphic,* an influential trilingual magazine promoting Swiss typography. He embodied the expansive precision of this movement. When asked about David Carson, postmodern designer and surfer, in 1996, Müller-Brockmann replied, "I don't surf, I dive."[1] His intense quest to achieve a universal system of communication calls to contemporary designers seeking ideal global forms for the world of new media.

1 See Kerry William Purcell, *Josef Müller-Brockmann* (New York: Phaidon Press, 2006), 277.

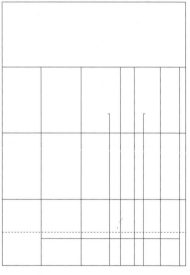

JOSEF MÜLLER-BROCKMANN
The "musica viva" poster is built up on a grid 4.5 fields wide and 4 fields deep. The two words "musica viva" are arranged in a cross, the letters of "musica" being set at irregular intervals so that a rhythm is produced. The lines of the program in small type align with the letters of "musica viva." In this way an impression is created of a severe but elegant architecture. Format: 128 x 90.5 cm, upright. Colors: blue-green-white.

Illustration and caption from *Grid Systems in Graphic Design* by Josef Müller-Brockmann.

GRID AND DESIGN PHILOSOPHY

JOSEF MÜLLER-BROCKMANN | 1981

The use of the grid as an ordering system is the expression of a certain mental attitude inasmuch as it shows that the designer conceives his work in terms that are constructive and oriented to the future.

This is the expression of a professional ethos: the designer's work should have the clearly intelligible, objective, functional, and aesthetic quality of mathematical thinking.

His work should thus be a contribution to general culture and itself form part of it.

Constructivist design that is capable of analysis and reproduction can influence and enhance the taste of a society and the way it conceives forms and colors. Design that is objective, committed to the common weal, well composed, and refined constitutes the basis of democratic behavior. Constructivist design means the conversion of design laws into practical solutions. Work done systematically and in accordance with strict formal principles makes those demands for directness, intelligibility, and the integration of all factors that are also vital in sociopolitical life.

Working with the grid system means submitting to laws of universal validity.

The use of the grid system implies the will to systematize, to clarify
the will to penetrate to the essentials, to concentrate
the will to cultivate objectivity instead of subjectivity
the will to rationalize the creative and technical production processes
the will to integrate elements of color, form, and material
the will to achieve architectural dominion over surface and space
the will to adopt a positive, forward-looking attitude
the recognition of the importance of education and the effect of work devised in a constructive and creative spirit.

Every visual creative work is a manifestation of the character of the designer. It is a reflection of his knowledge, his ability, and his mentality.

PAUL RAND MARRIED CREATIVE CONCEPT TO CLARITY OF FORM. The purpose of design was, he asserted, "to simplify, to clarify, to modify, to dignify, to dramatize, to persuade, and perhaps even to amuse."[1] Guided by European modernist principles, this son of Jewish Viennese immigrants pushed and pounded American graphic design for fifty years. In the 1940s, he led the concept-driven New Advertising movement in New York. Collaborative teams of art directors and copywriters still emulate the work he did with writer Bill Bernbach at the Weintraub Agency. Beginning in the 1950s he unified then-booming corporations with clean powerful marks, thus kicking off the maelstrom of corporate branding. His timeless logos for IBM, Westinghouse and ABC remain, testifying to the ability of their maker. In the latter half of his career Rand worked alone, preferring to communicate directly with the company president—no dilly-dallying with clients' committees and middlemen. Ultimately, he forged a relationship between graphic design and corporate America that carried designers to profitable professional heights, but left them dependent, perhaps troublingly, upon clients' societal visions and needs.

1 Paul Rand, "Form and Content," in *Design, Form, and Chaos* (New Haven: Yale University Press, 1993), 3.

GOOD DESIGN IS GOODWILL

PAUL RAND | 1987

Michelangelo, responding to the demands of Pope Julius II about the completion of the Sistine Ceiling, replied, "It will be finished when I shall have satisfied myself in the matter of art." "But it is our pleasure," retorted the pope, "that you should satisfy us in our desire to have it done quickly." And it was not until he was threatened with being thrown from the scaffolding that Michelangelo agreed to be more expeditious. On the whole, however, the relationship between Michelangelo and the pope was reciprocal. Mutual respect, apologies, and ducats were the means of mediation.

Today the relationship between designer (painter, writer, composer) and management shares certain similarities with that of our distinguished protagonists. What has always kept the designer and client at odds is the same thing that has kept them in accord. For the former, design is a means for invention and experiment, for the latter, a means of achieving economic, political, or social ends. But not all business people are aware that, in the words of a marketing professor at Northwestern University, "Design is a potent strategy tool that companies can use to gain a sustainable competitive advantage. Yet most companies neglect design as a strategy tool. What they don't realize is that design can enhance products, environments, communications, and corporate identity."

The expression "good design" came into usage circa 1940, when the Museum of Modern Art sponsored the exhibit "Useful Objects of American Design under Ten Dollars." The intention, of course, was to identify not just "good" design but the best, that which only the most skillful designer (trained or untrained) could produce. Over the years designers of both products and graphics have created an impressive collection of distinguished designs. Yet ironically, this body of good work makes one painfully aware of the abundance of poor design and the paucity of good designers. Talent is a rare commodity in the arts, as it is in other professions. But there is more to the story than this.

Even if it does not require extensive schooling, design is one of the most perplexing pursuits in which to excel. Besides the need for a God-given talent, the designer must contend with encyclopedic amounts of information, a seemingly endless stream of opinions, and the day-to-day problem of finding "new" ideas (popularly called "creativity").

Yet as a profession it is relatively easy to enter. Unlike those of architecture and engineering, it requires no accreditation (not that accreditation is always meaningful in the arts). It entails no authorization from official institutions, as do the legal and medical professions. (This is equally true of other arenas in the business world, for example, marketing and market research.) There is no set body of knowledge that must be mastered by the practitioners. What the designer and his client have in common is a license to practice without a license.

Many designers, schooled or self-taught, are interested primarily in things that look good and work well; they see their mission realized only when aesthetics and practical needs coalesce. What a designer does is not limited to any particular idea or form. Graphic design embraces every kind of problem of visual communication, from birth announcements to billboards. It embodies visual ideas, from the typography of a Shakespearean sonnet to the design and typography of a box of Kellogg's Corn Flakes. What might entitle these items to the "good design" accolade is their practicability and their beauty, both of which are embodied in the idea of quality. The Bahlsen design (circa 1930) meets both goals admirably. "H. Bahlsen, the biscuit maker of Hanover, was a manufacturer who combined art and his work in the most thorough fashion." He was one of those rare businessmen who believed that "art is the best means of propaganda."

Design is a personal activity and springs from the creative impulse of an individual. Group design or design by committee, although occasionally useful, deprives the designer of the distinct pleasure of personal accomplishment

PAUL RAND Logos: Westinghouse, 1960; IBM, 1962; UPS, 1961.

and self-realization. It may even hinder his or her thought processes, because work is not practiced under natural, tension-free conditions. Ideas have neither time to develop nor even the opportunity to occur. The tensions encountered in original work are different from those caused by discomfort or nervousness.

The relationship that exists between the designer and management is dichotomous. On the one hand, the designer is fiercely independent; on the other, he or she is dependent on management for support against bureaucracy and the caprice of the marketplace. I believe that design quality is proportionately related to the distance that exists between the designer and the management at the top. The closer this relationship, the more likely chances are for a meaningful design. For example, the relationship between the designer and the chief executive of Bahlsen was, undoubtedly, very close. "With a very few exceptions, all the Bahlsen wrappers are the work of a woman artist, Martel Schwichtenberg. In a masterly manner she contrived to keep the designs up to their original high standards."

Design is less a business than a calling. Many a designer's workday, in or out of the corporate environment, is ungoverned by a timesheet. Ideas, which are the designer's raison d'être, are not produced by whim or on the spur of the moment. Ideas are the lifeblood of any form of meaningful communication. But good ideas are obstinate and have a way of materializing only when and where they choose—in the shower or subway, in the morning or middle of the night. As if this weren't enough, an infinite number of people, with or without political motives, must scrutinize and pass on the designer's ideas. Most of these people, in management or otherwise, have no design background. They are not professionals who have the credentials to approve or disapprove the work of the professional designer, yet of course they do. There are rare exceptions—lay people who have an instinctive sense for design. Interestingly, these same people leave design to the experts.

If asked to pinpoint the reasons for the proliferation of poor design, I would probably have to conclude, all things being equal, that the difficulties lie with: (1) management's unawareness of or indifference to good design, (2) market researchers' vested interests, (3) designers' lack of authority or competence.

Real competence in the field of visual communication is something that only dedication, experience, and performance can validate. The roots of good design lie in aesthetics: painting, drawing, and architecture, while those of business and market research are in demographics and statistics; aesthetics and business are traditionally incompatible disciplines. The value judgments of the designer and the business executive are often at odds. Advertising executives and managers have their sights set on different goals: on costs and profits. "They are trained," says [Philip] Kotler, quoting a personnel executive, "in business schools to be numbers-oriented, to minimize risks, and to use analytical detached plans—not insights gained from hands-on experience. They are devoted to short-term returns and cost reduction, rather than developing long-term technological competitiveness. They prefer servicing existing markets rather than taking risks and developing new ones."

Many executives who spend time in a modern office at least eight hours a day may very well live in houses in which the latest audio equipment is hidden behind the doors of a Chippendale cabinet. Modern surroundings may be synonymous with work, but not with relaxation. The preference is for the traditional setting. (Most people are conditioned to prefer the fancy to the plain.) Design is seen merely as decoration—a legacy of the past. Quality and status are very often equated with traditional values, with costliness, with luxury. And in the comparatively rare instance that the business executive exhibits a preference for a modern home environment, it is usually the super modern, the lavish, and the extremely expensive. Design values for the pseudo-traditionalist or super-modernist are measured in extremes. For the former it is how old, for the latter how new. Good design is not based on nostalgia or trendiness. Intrinsic quality is the only real measure of good design.

In some circles art and design were, and still are, considered effeminate, something "removed from the common affairs of men." Others saw all artists "performing no useful function they could understand." At one time, design was even considered a woman's job. "Let men construct and women decorate," said Benn Pitman, the man who brought new ideas about the arts from England to the United States in the 1850s. To the businessman whose mind-set is only the bottom line, any reference to art or design is often an embarrassment. It implies waste and frivolity, having nothing to do with the serious business of business. To this person, art belongs, if anywhere, in the home or museum. Art is painting, sculpture, etching; design is wallpaper, carpeting, and upholstery patterns.

"'Art,'" says Henry James, "in our Protestant communities, where so many things have got so strangely twisted about, is supposed, in certain circles, to have some vaguely injurious effect on those who make it an important consideration.... It is assumed to be opposed in some mysterious manner to morality, to amusement, to instruction."

To many designers, art/design is a cultural mission in which life and work are inseparable. Clean surfaces, simple materials, and economy of means are the designer's articles of faith. Asceticism, rather than "the good life," motivates good designers—in keeping with the ideals of the modern painters, architects, and designers of the early part of this century, and with the beliefs, as expressed later by Edgar Kaufmann: good design is a "thorough merging of form and function and an awareness of human values, expressed in relation to industrial production for a democratic society."

Not just good design but the implication of its modernity needs to be stressed. Le Corbusier, the great and influential architect and theorist, commented: "To be modern is not a fashion, it is a state. It is necessary to understand history, and he who understands history knows how to find continuity between that which was, that which is, and that which will be."

[…]

Design no less than business poses ethical problems. A badly designed product that works is no less unethical than a beautiful product that doesn't. The former trivializes the consumer, the latter deceives him. Design that lacks ideas and depends entirely on form for its realization may possess a certain kind of mysterious charm; at the same time it may be uncommunicative. On the other hand, design that depends entirely on content will most likely be so tiresome that it will not compel viewing. "Idea and the form," says James, "are the needle and thread, and I never heard of a guild of tailors that recommended the use of thread without the needle or the needle without the thread." Good design satisfies both idea and form, the needle and the thread.

A company's reputation is very much affected by how the company appears and how its products work. A beautiful object that doesn't work is a reflection on the company's integrity. In the long run, it may lose not only customers but their goodwill. Good design will function no longer as the harbinger of good business but as the herald of hypocrisy. Beauty is a by-product of needs and functions. The Barcalounger is extremely comfortable, but it is an example of beauty gone astray. A consumer survey that would find such furniture comfortable might find it to be beautiful as well, merely because it is easy to conclude that if something works it must also be beautiful and vice versa. Ugliness is not a product of market research but of bad taste, of misreading opinions for analysis and information for ideas.

In 1907 the German Werkbund was formed, an organization whose purpose it was to forge the links between designer and manufacturer. It was intended to make the public aware of the folly of snobbery and to underscore

A DESIGN THAT IS COMPLEX, FUSSY, OR OBSCURE HARBORS A SELF-DESTRUCTIVE MECHANISM.

PAUL RAND
"Logos...Flags...
Street Signs"
1990

the significance of the "old ideals of simplicity, purity, and quality." Its aims were also to make producers aware of "a new sense of cultural responsibility, based on the recognition that men are molded by the objects that surround them."

From little buckslips to big buildings, the visual design problems of a large corporation are virtually without end. It is in the very solution of these problems—well-designed advertisements, packaging, products, and buildings—that a corporation is able to help shape its environment, to reach and to influence the taste of vast audiences. The corporation is in a singularly strategic position to heighten public awareness. Unlike routine philanthropic programs, this kind of contribution is a day-to-day activity that turns business strategy into social opportunity and good design into goodwill.

PAUL RAND Eye, Bee, M poster, 1981. Rand originally designed this rebus for an in-house IBM event, The Golden Circle Award. IBM forbid distribution, at first, worried that the design threatened their established graphic standards.

IN 1968 ROBERT VENTURI, DENISE SCOTT BROWN, STEVEN IZENOUR, AND A GROUP OF THEIR STUDENTS TOOK A TRIP TO LAS VEGAS. The trip was part of a studio class at Yale School of Art and Architecture. Out of this trip, a "postmodern manifesto"—*Learning from Las Vegas*—emerged.[1] This text attacked modern tenets with a postmodern embrace of pop culture and iconography. Privileging the commercial vernacular, Venturi et al. looked curiously at the Las Vegas Strip while withholding the more typical exclusionary judgments of modernism. As a result they observed that the modern world of "form follows function" had been dismembered. In Las Vegas, communication trumped function; graphic signs dominated architectural space. This recognition reoriented graphic designers and architects to a new postmodern world—a world of appropriation filled with irony, cliché, and pastiche: a world where, as Venturi says of Las Vegas, "If you take the signs away, there is no place."

1 For discussion of *Learning from Las Vegas* as postmodern manifesto, see Marianne DeKoven, *Utopia Limited: The Sixties and the Emergence of the Postmodern* (Durham: Duke University Press, 2004), 109-113.

LEARNING FROM LAS VEGAS
THE FORGOTTEN SYMBOLISM
OF ARCHITECTURAL FORM

ROBERT VENTURI, DENISE SCOTT BROWN, AND STEVEN IZENOUR | 1972

A SIGNIFICANCE FOR A&P PARKING LOTS,
OR LEARNING FROM LAS VEGAS

Substance for a writer consists not merely of those realities he thinks he discovers; it consists even more of those realities that have been made available to him by the literature and idioms of his own day and by the images that still have vitality in the literature of the past. Stylistically, a writer can express his feeling about this substance either by imitation, if it sits well with him, or by parody, if it doesn't.

Learning from the existing landscape is a way of being revolutionary for an architect. Not the obvious way, which is to tear down Paris and begin again, as Le Corbusier suggested in the 1920s, but another, more tolerant way; that is, to question how we look at things.

The commercial strip, the Las Vegas Strip in particular—the example par excellence—challenges the architect to take a positive, non-chip-on-the-shoulder view. Architects are out of the habit of looking nonjudgmentally at the environment, because orthodox Modern architecture is progressive, if not revolutionary, utopian, and puristic; it is dissatisfied with existing conditions. Modern architecture has been anything but permissive: Architects have preferred to change the existing environment rather than enhance what is there.

But to gain insight from the commonplace is nothing new: Fine art often follows folk art. Romantic architects of the eighteenth century discovered an existing and conventional rustic architecture. Early Modern architects appropriated an existing and conventional industrial vocabulary without much adaptation. Le Corbusier loved grain elevators and steamships; the Bauhaus looked like a factory; Mies refined the details of American steel factories for concrete buildings. Modern architects work through analogy, symbol, and image—although they have gone to lengths to disclaim almost all determinants of their forms except structural necessity and the program—and they derive insights, analogies, and stimulation from unexpected images. There is a perversity in the learning process: We look backward at history and tradition to go forward; we can also look downward to go upward. And withholding judgment may be used as a tool to make later judgment more sensitive. This is a way of learning from everything.

COMMERCIAL VALUES AND COMMERCIAL METHODS

Las Vegas is analyzed here only as a phenomenon of architectural communication. Just as an analysis of the structure of a Gothic cathedral need not include a debate on the morality of medieval religion, so Las Vegas's values are not questioned here. The morality of commercial advertising, gambling, interests, and the competitive instinct is not at issue here, although, indeed, we believe it should be in the architect's broader, *synthetic* tasks of which an analysis such as this is but one aspect. The analysis of a drive-in church in this context would match that of a drive-in restaurant, because this is a study of method, not content. Analysis of one of the architectural variables in isolation from the others is a respectable scientific and humanistic activity, so long as all are resynthesized in design. Analysis of existing American urbanism is a socially desirable activity to the extent that it teaches us architects to be more understanding and less authoritarian in the plans we make for both inner-city renewal and new development. In addition, there is no reason why the methods of commercial persuasion and the skyline of signs analyzed here should not serve the purpose of civic and cultural enhancement. But this is not entirely up to the architect.

BILLBOARDS ARE ALMOST ALL RIGHT

Architects who can accept the lessons of primitive vernacular architecture, so easy to take in an exhibit like "Architecture without Architects," and of industrial, vernacular architecture, so easy to adapt to an electronic and space

NAKED CHILDREN HAVE NEVER PLAYED IN *OUR* FOUNTAINS, AND I. M. PEI WILL NEVER BE HAPPY ON ROUTE 66.

ROBERT VENTURI,
DENISE SCOTT BROWN,
AND STEVEN IZENOUR
*Learning from Las Vegas:
The Forgotten Symbolism
of Architectural Form*
1977

vernacular as elaborate neo-Brutalist or neo-Constructivist megastructures, do not easily acknowledge the validity of the commercial vernacular. For the artist, creating the new may mean choosing the old or the existing. Pop artists have relearned this. Our acknowledgment of existing, commercial architecture at the scale of the highway is within this tradition.

Modern architecture has not so much excluded the commercial vernacular as it has tried to take it over by inventing and enforcing a vernacular of its own, improved and universal. It has rejected the combination of fine art and crude art. The Italian landscape has always harmonized the vulgar and the Vitruvian: the *contorni* around the duomo, the *portiere's* laundry across the *padrone's portone*, *Supercortemaggiore* against the Romanesque apse. Naked children have never played in our fountains, and I. M. Pei will never be happy on Route 66.

ARCHITECTURE AS SPACE

Architects have been bewitched by a single element of the Italian landscape: the piazza. Its traditional, pedestrian-scaled, and intricately enclosed space is easier to like than the spatial sprawl of Route 66 and Los Angeles. Architects have been brought up on space, and enclosed space is the easiest to handle. During the last forty years, theorists of Modern architecture (Wright and Le Corbusier sometimes excepted) have focused on space as the essential ingredient that separates architecture from painting, sculpture, and literature. Their definitions glory in the uniqueness of the medium; although sculpture and painting may sometimes be allowed spatial characteristics, sculptural or pictorial architecture is unacceptable—because space is sacred.

Purist architecture was partly a reaction against nineteenth-century eclecticism. Gothic churches, Renaissance banks, and Jacobean manors were frankly picturesque. The mixing of styles meant the mixing of media. Dressed in historical styles, buildings evoked explicit associations and romantic allusions to the past to convey literary, ecclesiastical, national, or programmatic symbolism. Definitions of architecture as space and form at the service of program and structure were not enough. The overlapping of disciplines may have diluted the architecture, but it enriched the meaning.

Modern architects abandoned a tradition of iconology in which painting, sculpture, and graphics were combined with architecture. The delicate hieroglyphics on a bold pylon, the archetypal inscriptions of a Roman architrave, the mosaic processions in Sant' Apollinare, the ubiquitous tattoos over a Giotto Chapel, the enshrined hierarchies around a Gothic portal, even the illusionistic frescoes in a Venetian villa, all contain messages beyond their

Map of Las Vegas strip.

ornamental contribution to architectural space. The integration of the arts in Modern architecture has always been called a good thing. But one did not paint on Mies. Painted panels were floated independently of the structure by means of shadow joints; sculpture was in or near but seldom on the building. Objects of art were used to reinforce architectural space at the expense of their own content. The Kolbe in the Barcelona Pavilion was a foil to the directed spaces: The message was mainly architectural. The diminutive signs in most Modern buildings contained only the most necessary messages, like LADIES, minor accents begrudgingly applied.

ARCHITECTURE AS SYMBOL

Critics and historians, who documented the "decline of popular symbols" in art, supported orthodox Modern architects, who shunned symbolism of form as an expression or reinforcement of content: Meaning was to be communicated, not through allusion to previously known forms, but through the inherent, physiognomic characteristics of form. The creation of architectural form was to be a logical process, free from images of past experience, determined solely by program and structure, with an occasional assist, as Alan Colquhoun has suggested, from intuition.

But some recent critics have questioned the possible level of content to be derived from abstract forms. Others have demonstrated that the functionalists, despite their protestations, derived a formal vocabulary of their own, mainly from current art movements and the industrial vernacular; and latter-day followers such as the Archigram group have turned, while similarly protesting, to Pop Art and the space industry. However, most critics have slighted a continuing iconology in popular commercial art, the persuasive heraldry that pervades our environment from the advertising of the New Yorker to the superbillboards of Houston. And their theory of the "debasement" of symbolic architecture in nineteenth-century eclecticism has blinded them to the value of the representational architecture along highways. Those who acknowledge this roadside eclecticism denigrate it, because it flaunts the cliché of a decade ago as well as the style of a century ago. But why not? Time travels fast today.

The Miami Beach Modern motel on a bleak stretch of highway in southern Delaware reminds jaded drivers of the welcome luxury of a tropical resort, persuading them, perhaps, to forgo the gracious plantation across the Virginia border called Motel Monticello. The real hotel in Miami alludes to the international stylishness of a Brazilian resort, which, in turn, derives from the International Style of middle Corbu. This evolution from the high source through the middle source to the low source took only thirty years. Today, the middle source, the neo-eclectic architecture of the 1940s and the 1950s, is less interesting than its commercial adaptations. Roadside copies of Ed Stone are more interesting than the real Ed Stone.

SYMBOL IN SPACE BEFORE FORM IN SPACE: LAS VEGAS AS A COMMUNICATION SYSTEM

The sign for the Motel Monticello, a silhouette of an enormous Chippendale highboy, is visible on the highway before the motel itself. This architecture of styles and signs is antispatial; it is an architecture of communication over space; communication dominates space as an element in the architecture and in the landscape. But it is for a new scale of landscape. The philosophical associations of the old eclecticism evoked subtle and complex meanings to be savored in the docile spaces of a traditional landscape. The commercial persuasion of roadside eclecticism provokes bold impact in the vast and complex setting of a new landscape of big spaces, high speeds, and complex programs. Styles and signs make connections among many elements, far apart and seen fast. The message is basely commercial; the context is basically new.

A driver thirty years ago could maintain a sense of orientation in space. At the simple crossroad a little sign with an arrow confirmed what was obvious. One knew where one was. When the crossroads becomes a cloverleaf, one must turn right to turn left. […] But the driver has no time to ponder paradoxical subtleties within a dangerous, sinuous maze. He or she relies on signs for guidance—enormous signs in vast spaces at high speeds.

The dominance of signs over space at a pedestrian scale occurs in big airports. Circulation in a big railroad station required little more than a simple axial system from taxi to train, by ticket window, stores, waiting room, and platform—all virtually without signs. Architects object to signs in buildings: "If the plan is clear, you can see where to go." But complex programs and settings require complex combinations of media beyond the purer architectural triad of structure, form, and light at the service of space. They suggest an architecture of bold communication rather than one of subtle expression.

THE ARCHITECTURE OF PERSUASION

The cloverleaf and airport communicate with moving crowds in cars or on foot for efficiency and safety. But words and symbols may be used in space for commercial persuasion. The Middle Eastern bazaar contains no signs; the Strip is virtually all signs. In the bazaar, communication works through proximity. Along its narrow aisles, buyers feel and smell the merchandise, and the merchant applies explicit oral persuasion. In the narrow streets of the medieval town, although signs occur, persuasion is mainly through the sight and smell of the real cakes through the doors and windows of the bakery. On Main Street, shop-window displays for pedestrians along the sidewalks and exterior signs, perpendicular to the street for motorists, dominate the scene almost equally.

On the commercial strip the supermarket windows contain no merchandise. There may be signs announcing the day's bargains, but they are to be read by pedestrians approaching from the parking lot. The building itself is set back from the highway and half hidden, as is most of the urban environment, by parked cars. The vast parking lot is in front, not at the rear, since it is a symbol as well as a convenience. The building is low because air conditioning demands low spaces, and merchandising techniques discourage second floors; its architecture is neutral because it can hardly be seen from the road. Both merchandise and architecture are disconnected from the road. The big sign leaps to connect the driver to the store, and down the road the cake mixes and detergents are advertised by their national manufacturers on enormous billboards inflected toward the highway. The graphic sign in space has become the architecture of this landscape. Inside, the A&P has reverted to the bazaar except that graphic packaging has replaced the oral persuasion of the merchant. At another scale, the shopping center off the highway returns in its pedestrian malls to the medieval street.

VAST SPACE IN THE HISTORICAL TRADITION AND AT THE A&P

The A&P parking lot is a current phase in the evolution of vast space since Versailles. The space that divides high-speed highway and low, sparse buildings produces no enclosure and little direction. To move through a piazza is to move between high enclosing forms. To move through this landscape is to move over vast expansive texture: the megatexture of the commercial landscape. The parking lot is the *parterre* of the asphalt landscape. The patterns of parking lines give direction much as the paving patterns, curbs, borders, and *tapis vert* give direction in Versailles; grids of lamp posts substitute for obelisks, rows of urns, and statues as points of identity and continuity in the vast space. But it is the highway signs, through their sculptural forms or pictorial silhouettes, their particular positions in space, their inflected shapes, and their graphic meanings, that identify and unify the megatexture. They make verbal and symbolic connections through space, communicating a

TO FIND OUR SYMBOLISM WE MUST GO TO THE SUBURBAN EDGES OF THE EXISTING CITY.... THEN THE ARCHETYPAL LOS ANGELES WILL BE OUR ROME AND LAS VEGAS OUR FLORENCE.

ROBERT VENTURI,
DENISE SCOTT BROWN,
AND STEVEN IZENOUR
*Learning from Las Vegas:
The Forgotten Symbolism
of Architectural Form*
1977

complexity of meanings through hundreds of associations in few seconds from far away. Symbol dominates space. Architecture is not enough. Because the spatial relationships are made by symbols more than by forms, architecture in this landscape becomes symbol in space, rather than form in space. Architecture defines very little: The big sign and the little building is the rule of Route 66.

The sign is more important than the architecture. This is reflected in the proprietor's budget. The sign at the front of a vulgar extravaganza, the buildings at the back, a modest necessity. The architecture is what is cheap. Sometimes the building is the sign: The duck store in the shape of a duck, called "The Long Island Duckling," is sculptural symbol and architectural shelter. Contradiction between outside and inside was common in architecture before the modern movement, particularly in urban and monumental architecture. Baroque domes were symbols as well as spatial constructions, and they are bigger in scale and higher outside than inside in order to dominate their urban setting and communicate their symbolic message. The false fronts of Western stores did the same thing: They were bigger and taller than the interiors they fronted to communicate the store's importance and to enhance the quality and unity of the street. But false fronts are of the order and scale of Main Street. From the desert town on the highway in the West of today, we can learn new and vivid lessons about an impure architecture of communication. The little low buildings, gray-brown like the desert, separate and recede from the street that is now the highway, their false fronts disengaged and turned perpendicular to the highway as big, high signs. If you take the signs away, there is no place. The desert town is intensified communication along the highway.

WOLFGANG WEINGART TURNED A REBELLIOUS EYE TO SWISS RATIONAL TYPOGRAPHY, RESCUING IT FROM WHAT HE DESCRIBES AS "THE THRESHOLD OF STAGNATION." While studying under the Swiss masters, Armin Hofman and Emil Ruder at the Künstgewerbeschule in Basel in the 1960s, Weingart reacted to existing standards by pushing typography to the limits of legibility and beyond. He narrowly escaped expulsion. Combining extreme letterspacing, slant, weight, size, and repetition with a fierce practical knowledge of printing, Weingart dismantled the rational methodology of his elders. Out of this radicality emerged a design movement appropriate to the changing postmodern times. New Wave was born. Weingart and the students he later taught at the Künstgewerbeschule in the sixties, seventies, and eighties, including April Greiman and Dan Friedman, used their intimate knowledge of Swiss modernism to open its unrelenting structure to the dynamic experiments of a new era. His audacity urges us to look deeply at our own time and, in so doing, "to question established typography standards, change the rules, and to reevaluate its potential."[1]

1 Wolfgang Weingart, *My Way to Typography*, trans. Katherine Wolff and Catherine Schelbert (Baden: Lars Müller, 2000), 112.

MY WAY TO TYPOGRAPHY

WOLFGANG WEINGART | 2000

FOURTH INDEPENDENT PROJECT: LETTERS AND TYPOGRAPHIC ELEMENTS IN A NEW CONTEXT

In an era when lead type was virtually obsolete, the environment of a traditionally equipped type shop—its elements and tools in metal, wood, or synthetic materials—was the context, in fact, the impetus that enabled me to develop a progressive curriculum for the Künstgewerbeschule Basel.

Swiss typography in general, and the typography of the Basel school in particular, played an important international role from the fifties until the end of the sixties. Its development, however, was on the threshold of stagnation; it became sterile and anonymous. My vision, fundamentally compatible with our school's philosophy, was to breathe new life into the teaching of typography by reexamining the assumed principles of its current practice.

The only way to break typographic rules was to know them. I acquired this advantage during my apprenticeship as I became expert in letterpress printing. I assigned my students exercises that not only addressed basic design relationships with type placement, size, and weight, but also encouraged them to critically analyze letterspacing to experiment with the limits of readability.

We discovered that as increased space was inserted between letters, the
words or word groups became graphic in expression, and that understanding
the message was less dependent upon reading than we had supposed.

Our activities challenged the viewpoint of Emil Ruder and his followers. In
the mid-sixties he wrote a succinct manifesto, a part of which I typographically
interpreted for the cover of *Typographische Monatsblätter*, Number 5/1973:

"Typography has one plain duty before it and that is to convey information
in writing. No argument or consideration can absolve typography from this
duty. A printed work that cannot be read becomes a product without purpose.
More than graphic design, typography is an expression of technology, precision, and good order."

Founded by Emil Ruder and Armin Hofmann, the Weiterbildungsklasse
für Graphik, the international Advanced Program for Graphic Design, was
scheduled to begin in April 1968. Ruder's heartfelt wish was to teach typography, but because of additional obligations as the school director, he would
need a teaching assistant. He asked me, and I readily accepted. Tragically, his
unexpected illness and regular hospital confinements in Basel precluded the
chance of ever working together.

The first seven students came from the United States, Canada, England,
and Switzerland, expecting to study with the masters Hofmann and Ruder.
When I showed up as the typography teacher, their shock was obvious. Because of my training and radical experiments, and because we were around the
same age, the students began to trust me. Eventually, disappointment gave
way to curiosity.

The teachers agreed on common themes for the initial two years of
the advanced program, the symbol and the package. Feeling more confident
by the second year, bolstered by the students' enthusiasm, I risked further
experimentation, and my classes became a laboratory to test and expand
models for a new typography.

It was a major undertaking to organize my extremely diverse typographic
ideas when I was asked to exhibit at the Stuttgart gallery Knauer-Expo in
December 1969. I designed eleven broadsides relating to thoughts and fanta-
sies about my life. One of them, entitled "was ich morgen am liebsten machen
würde" (what I would most like to do tomorrow), was a list of wishes and
dreams, and it has become one of my favorite works.

Accelerated by the social unrest of our generation, the force behind Swiss
typography and its philosophy of reduction was losing its international hold.
My students were inspired, we were on to something different, and we knew it.
[…]

FIFTH INDEPENDENT PROJECT: TYPOGRAPHY
AS ENDLESS REPETITION

Years after our explosive rebellion against the prevailing status of Swiss typography and all the values that it had come to embody, my work, too, became repetitive. Disheartening as it was, I had to admit that our school type shop, although well stocked in metal type, rule lines, symbols, and ornaments, flexible in all possible techniques, no longer offered creative potential, not for me personally and not in the professional practice of design.

Since the invention of printing, typography had been the domain of craftsmen. The artists and designers of the twenties and thirties, the so-called pioneers of modern typography, El Lissitzky, Kurt Schwitters, Piet Zwart, whose work anticipated a future direction in graphic design, perhaps came to a similar dead end due to the inherent limitations of perpendicular composition in lead typography.

In my case the crisis came at the beginning of the seventies when the student unrest had subsided, when many of us were trying to envision a new life. The renewed challenge to find other possibilities in my work, to find my way out of a leaden typographic cage, seemed futile.

It was too soon to imagine the potential of layering lithographic films. Nor could I predict that in the darkroom another world of surprise awaited: transparency and superimposed dot screens.

From a feeling of nowhere to go, a low point and a standstill, I set repeated, single type elements. The pictures conjured up many associations: the endless expanse of the desert, the steps of archaeological sites, the discipline of my apprenticeship, and, from childhood, the drudgery of survival in a postwar economy and a report card with the failing grade that would never improve—in Germany, the number 1. Lines that spanned a double-page spread reminded me of first grade in Salem Valley and my practice notebook for handwriting. The word "schön," set in bold with two fine points above it, defined my idea of beauty. The rows of Rs were elephants with their long trunks, a peaceable herd roaming a dry river valley at the foot of a steep mountain massif. The cross, the registration mark of the printer, was the intersection of north, south, east, and west. The letter Y was a dichotomy, the arid desert strewn with colorful tulips. Pages of bold points and vertical lines were abstractions of photographs brought back from journeys in the Near East.

This phase of my work may well have been influenced by Serial Art, or by Repetition Typography practiced in the class of Emil Ruder during the sixties. The typeface Univers designed by Adrian Frutiger of Switzerland, a longtime

I WAS MOTIVATED TO PROVOKE THE STODGY PROFESSION AND TO STRETCH THE TYPE SHOP'S CAPABILITIES TO THE BREAKING POINT, AND, FINALLY, TO PROVE ONCE AGAIN THAT TYPOGRAPHY IS AN ART.

WOLFGANG
WEINGART
*My Way
to Typography*
2000

schon schon schon schon
schon schon schon schon
schon schon schon schon
schon schon schon schon
schon schon schon schon
schon schon schon schon
schon schon schon schon
schon schon schon schon

WOLFGANG WEINGART Example of typographic experiments at Basel School of Design, 1968-1971. Weingart notes, "The word 'schön,' set in bold with two fine points above it, defined my idea of beauty."

friend of Ruder, offered Basel a progressive approach to the arrangement of typography. The design of Univers was ideal for Ruder's own typographic work and that of his students, especially favored by Hans-Rudolf Lutz who studied at the Basel school for one year from 1963 to 1964. Lutz and a few of his colleagues designed typographic pictures that would have been difficult to compose in any other typeface.

Since the invention of book printing, Univers was the first entire font system to be designed with interchangeable weights, proportions, and corresponding italics. In the design of older typefaces visual alignment among such variations was not a standard consideration. For a given size of type all twenty-one variations of Univers, whether light, regular, medium, bold, condensed, expanded, or italic, had the same X-height (the height of lowercase letters without ascenders or descenders) and the same baseline. This simplified letterpress printing and increased the possibilities for visual contrast in tone, weight, width, and direction, available in eleven sizes for metal typesetting.

When I came to the Basel School of Design the coarse Berthold Akzidenz-Grotesk, so rarely used, was fast asleep in the type drawer under a blanket of dust. I woke it up.

KATHERINE McCOY GALVANIZED THE DESIGN COMMUNITY DURING THE LATE 1970S AND 1980S. UNDER HER LEADERSHIP, EXPERIMENTAL WORK UNDERTAKEN AT CRANBROOK ACADEMY OF ART IN MICHIGAN TRANSFORMED GRAPHIC DESIGN INTO PROVOCATION. Balking against the modern constraints of Swiss typographic systems, her students ushered in a period of complexity, ambiguity, and subjectivity. Moving beyond the more formal radical experimentation of Wolfgang Weingart, McCoy explored "new relationships between text and image." The resulting multilayered, personal work consciously provoked interpretation from the audience. Modernism's emphasis on form gave way to a highly individuated study of expression. Typography became discourse to be evaluated and discussed within the dense cultural context of philosophy, linguistics, and cultural theory. Angry modernists protested the work as "ugly" and "impractical," kicking off the "Legibility Wars" of the 1990s. This uproar drives home the importance of Cranbrook. The work at this small rustbelt school forced the modern tenets underlying our profession to the surface. There they could be critically examined and addressed through fresh postmodern eyes.

TYPOGRAPHY AS DISCOURSE

KATHERINE McCOY WITH DAVID FREJ | 1988

The recent history of graphic design in the United States reveals a series of actions and reactions. The fifties saw the flowering of U.S. graphic design in the New York School. This copy-concept and image-oriented direction was challenged in the sixties by the importation of Swiss minimalism, a structural and typographic system that forced a split between graphic design and advertising. Predictably, designers in the next decade rebelled against Helvetica and the grid system that had become the official American corporate style.

In the early seventies, Robert Venturi's *Complexity and Contradiction in Architecture* emerged alongside the study of graphic design history as influences on American graphic design students. Simultaneously, Switzerland's Basel school was transformed by Wolfgang Weingart's syntactical experimentation, an enthusiasm that quickly spread to U.S. schools. Academia's rediscovery of early-twentieth-century Modernism, the appearance of historicized and vernacular architectural postmodernism, and the spread of Weingartian structural expressionism all came together in the graphic explosion labeled as New Wave.

Shattering the constraints of minimalism was exhilarating and far more fun than the antiseptic discipline of the classical Swiss school. After a brief flurry of diatribes in the graphic design press, this permissive new approach quickly moved into the professional mainstream. Today, however, the maverick has been tamed, codified into a formalistic style that fills our design annuals with endlessly sophisticated renditions. What was originally a revolution is now an institution, as predictable as Beaux Arts architecture. It is the new status quo—the New Academy, as Phil Meggs calls it.

Determining whether New Wave is postmodernism or just late Modernism is important in understanding new work today. New Wave extends the classical Swiss interest in structure to dissections and recombinations of graphic design's grammar. Layered images and textures continue the collage aesthetic begun by Cubism, Constructivism, and Dada. But the addition of vernacular imagery and colors reflects postmodern architecture's discovery of popular culture, and the reintroduction of the classic serif typefaces draws on pre-twentieth-century history. Taken as a whole, however, New Wave's complex arrangements are largely syntactical, abstracting type and images into baroquely Modern compositions.

The New Academy's knowing, often slick iterations have left some graphic designers dissatisfied. As a result, long-neglected design elements, such as semantic expression in form, text, and imagery, are beginning to resurface. Much of this recent work steps outside the lineage of Bauhaus/Basel/New Wave, and, not surprisingly, some of its practitioners come from fine art, photographic, or literary backgrounds rather than graphic design training.

When one looks for experimental typography today, what one finds is not so much new typography as new relationships between text and image. In fact, the typography so celebrated over the past ten years of structuralist dissection is disappearing. The look and structure of the letter is underplayed, and verbal signification, interacting with imagery and symbols, is instead relied upon. The best new work is often aformal and sometimes decidedly anti-formal, despite the presence of some New Wave elements. Reacting to the technical perfection of mainstream graphic design, refinement and mastery are frequently rejected in favor of the directness of unmannered, hand-drawn, or vernacular forms—after all, technical expertise is hardly a revelation anymore. These designers value expression over style.

Here on the edges of graphic design, the presence of the designer is sometimes so oblique that certain pieces would seem to spring directly from our popular culture. Reflecting current linguistic theory, the notion of "authorship" as a personal, formal vocabulary is less important than the dialogue between the graphic object and its audience; no longer are there one-way statements from designers. The layering of content, as opposed to New Wave's

KATHERINE McCOY AND
MICHAEL McCOY
*The New Cranbrook
Design Discourse*
1990

formal layering of collage elements, is the key to this exchange. Objective communication is enhanced by deferred meanings, hidden stories, and alternative interpretations.

Sources for much current experimentation can be traced to recent fine art and photography, and to literary and art criticism. Influenced by French poststructuralism, critics and artists deconstruct verbal language as a filter or bias that inescapably manipulates the reader's response. When this approach is applied to art and photography, form is treated as a visual language to be read as well as seen. Both the texts and the images are to be read in detail, their meanings decoded. Clearly, this intellectualized communication asks a lot of its audience; this is harder work than the formal pleasures of New Wave.

Much new typography is very quiet. Some of the most interesting, in fact, is impossible to show here because of its radically modest scale or its subtle development through a sequence of pages. Some is bold in scale but so matter-of-fact that it makes little in the way of a visual statement. (One designer calls these strictly linguistic intentions "nonallusive" typography.) Typefaces now range from the classics to banal, often industrial sans serifs. Copy is often treated as just that—undifferentiated blocks of words—without the mannered manipulations of New Wave, where sentences and words are playfully exploded to express their parts. Text is no longer the syntactic playground of Weingart's descendants.

These cryptic, poker-faced juxtapositions of text and image do not always strive for elegance or refinement, although they may achieve it inadvertently. The focus now is on expression through semantic content, utilizing the intellectual software of visual language as well as the structural hardware and graphic grammar of Modernism. It is an interactive process that—as art always anticipates social evolution—heralds our emerging information economy, in which meanings are as important as materials.

LORRAINE WILD EMERGED OUT OF THE EXPERIMENTAL, THEORETICAL WORLD OF CRANBROOK
ACADEMY OF ART'S DESIGN PROGRAM, RUN BY MICHAEL McCOY AND KATHERINE McCOY.
As head of the California Institute of the Arts' visual communication program from 1985 to 1991, Wild worked
furiously to revamp graphic design education. There she boldly confronted the insular objectivity of modernist
design education. Students, she maintains, must "see themselves within the historical continuum of visual and
verbal communication." In this excerpt from a larger essay, Wild questions her own earlier assertions of conceptual, verbal skills as the key to training future designers. Instead, she suggests, in our post-postmodern world
we should take another look at form, moving beyond past considerations of technique into something more
complex yet also elemental, which she terms "craft." "A new commitment to the practice of craft," she asserts,
"will supplement design theory and help reposition design at the center of what designers contribute to the
culture." Across her career, Wild has been one of design's clearest voices of critical and historical inquiry; at the
same time, her visual work has embodied a passion for typographic detail and formal invention and analysis.

THE MACRAMÉ OF RESISTANCE

LORRAINE WILD | 1998

CRAFT

Instead of technique, I think it might be useful to talk about craft. A contemporary mistake assumes that craft has something to do with papier-mâché, or
that it is merely the manipulation of production. It is true that the more one
understands the computer or printing, the better one can devise solutions to
problems. But to define craft trivially, only in terms of technique, does not
address the way that knowledge is developed through skill.

My own interest in craft stems from my experience as a design student at
Cranbrook, where "the crafts," like weaving and ceramics and metal smithing,
were taught seriously. I was always confused by what seemed like a strict but
unexplained wall between design and craft; "craft" seemed to be limited to the
making of one-of-a-kind things, whereas design was aimed at mass production. We all made things for use, but a deeper issue seemed to exist at the heart
of how things were made.

In my search to understand this, I encountered *The Art of the Maker*, a
book by the late British design theorist Peter Dormer.[1] He discusses craft in
terms of two different types of knowledge. The first is theoretical knowledge,
the concepts behind things, the language we use to describe and understand
ideas; the second is tacit knowledge, knowledge gained through experience,
or "know-how."

1 Peter Dormer, *The Art of the
Maker: Skill and Its Meaning in
Art, Craft, and Design* (London:
Thames and Hudson, 1994),
11-13.

LORRAINE WILD
"The Macramé
of Resistance"
1998

The tacit knowledge required to make something work is not the same as a theoretical understanding of the principles behind it. Theory might help you understand how to make something better, but craft knowledge (sometimes also called "local" knowledge) has to be experienced on another level. For Dormer, these two types of knowledge are completely intertwined.

Much of craft defies description. "Craft knowledge" is acquired by accumulating experience, and as you attain mastery you don't think so much about the conceptual basis that got you where you're going. Craft knowledge, though hard to get, achieves the status of a skill once it is taken for granted and not rethought every time it has to be put into use. It's instinctual.

Knowledge gained through familiarity also includes that which we know through the senses, connoisseurship, recognition based on not only attribution or classification but also just knowing what is good (having "an eye"). Craft knowledge has to stand up to public scrutiny, but it's also very personal because it has been gained through direct experience.

When craft is put into the framework of graphic design, this might constitute what is meant by the "designer's voice"—that part of a design that is not industriously addressing the ulterior motives of a project, but instead follows the inner agenda of the designer's craft. This guides the "body of work" of a designer over and beyond the particular goal of each project. So craft is about tactics and concepts, seeking opportunities in the gaps of what is known, rather than trying to organize everything in a unifying theory. As Dormer states, "One needs the ability to experiment. Experimenting,…often described as playing around, demands judgment—it improves one's sense of discrimination." Dormer saw the search that is part of craft as a critical human function, comparing it to processes like the creative thinking practiced by mathematicians or physicists at the top of their games. Dormer claimed the activity of craft as a major part of our culture.

Thinking about this larger definition of craft, which equates investigation with meaning, it's possible to better account for the individual visions of many graphic designers who have produced bodies of work that don't seem so stuck in the limitations of the market. Too personal, maybe, or too eccentric, their work resonates anyway, looks better and better over time, and makes more sense. I look at my own list of guilty pleasures, designers whose work I love because of its integrity to itself, above all else, like W. A. Dwiggins, who reinvented American typography by bringing arts-and-crafts values to design for machine production, all the while running his completely hand-crafted puppet theater out of a garage in Massachusetts; or Alvin Lustig, an architect, printer, designer, educator, who refused to specialize (he is the author of one of my favorite definitions of design: "I propose solutions that nobody wants to problems that don't exist"); or Imre Reiner, an anti-Modernist typographer in Switzerland, who rebelled against "objectivity" by coupling his own beautifully subjective scrawl with the public language of classical typography; or Sister Corita Kent, Southern California nun and printmaker who, in the 1960s, seized upon the idea of using the language of pop culture to speak to her local audience about spirituality, subverting and appropriating to communicate before those words were in our critical vocabularies; or Big Daddy Roth, and this I really can't explain, except that I think it has something to do with the pure audaciousness and delight of thinking and acting really locally; or Edward Fella, who mutated out of "commercial art" by working on problems only as he defined them—his commitment to anti-mastery (exemplified by his dictum: "keep the irregularities inconsistent") liberates design from digital perfection, getting down with everyday life, creating poetry.

Each of these designers invents in ways that transcend the clichés of "concept" that characterize so many of the current predictions of what design needs for the future. It's too easy to write this work off because of its marginality, but we need to pay attention because it suggests an alternative path. As another writer on the subject of craft, Malcolm McCullough, in his book *Abstracting Craft*, has stated, "The meaning of our work is connected to how it is made, not just 'concepted.'" I am highly self-conscious of the weirdness, in 1998, of arguing for a reenergized and reinvented teaching of basic color theory, or drawing, or composition, or basic typography that reconnects the digital with the whole span of graphic invention. But these are the tools we need to build creative independence, to liberate invention, to produce the exceptional.

A new commitment to the practice of craft will supplement design theory and help reposition design at the center of what designers contribute to the culture (and to commerce, in the long run). This is what is missing from all of the predictions for the future of design as a purely conceptual or technical activity. It's frustrating to watch so many attempt to reduce design to a theoretical argument, undervaluing the knowledge and pleasure to be gained by passionate engagement in the craft itself. The knowledge gained through activities that can be described as tactical, everyday, or simply craft is powerful and important, and it must form the foundation of a designer's education and work—it is how we create ideas; again, how we create culture. Why else are we here?

FOR MORE THAN THIRTY YEARS PAULA SCHER HAS CREATED POWERFUL GRAPHIC DESIGN. SHE IS KNOWN FOR HER EXPRESSIVE USE OF TYPOGRAPHY, AN APPROACH THAT SHE BEGAN TO DEVELOP IN THE 1970S, EARLY IN HER CAREER. During this period Scher designed covers for CBS and Atlantic Records. In 1991 she became the first female partner at Pentagram, New York. Despite this milestone, Scher emphatically does not consider herself a feminist. In fact, Scher's pragmatic streak tends to veer away from the more theoretical and political side of the profession. The essay below was written in 1989, a period in which clashes between form and content, modernism and postmodernism, began to heat up. Appropriately, her essay is not a complex intellectual exploration but states her own personal theory of creativity and maturation. Scher reminds us of the core of all of our work: the creative act itself.

THE DARK IN THE MIDDLE OF THE STAIRS

PAULA SCHER | 1989

One morning, my snotty twenty-two-year-old assistant danced into the studio and informed me that he went to the opening of some graphic design competition and I only had one piece in the show.

"Was it a good show?" I asked. "Yeah, it was okay," he said. "There was a lot of work from a guy in Iowa who sort of looks like Duffy Design."

I harrumphed and muttered, "Too much style and no substance."

I've been muttering "too much style and no substance" frequently for the past several years. I love muttering it and I hear all kinds of people I respect and admire mutter it. Our great designer "institutions" mutter it a lot. I've noticed that it's usually muttered in relation to designers who are younger than the mutterer. "Too much style and no substance" is often coupled with "a flash in the pan" as a way of describing hot young designers who get more than one piece in a design show.

What a wonderful way to demean youth! "Too much style" helps us conceal that nagging inkling we have that our own work may be out of style, and "no substance" convinces us that our potentially dated work is somehow more meaningful, rendering style irrelevant. Sometimes, it is even true.

But what all this muttering denies is the great excitement in finding and creating style, that thrill in putting the pieces together in a way that looks new and fresh, if not to the design community at large, then at least to ourselves.

PAULA SCHER
Interview with
Ellen Lupton
1995

These are the kind of discoveries we generally make early in our careers, when each design is a new experience for us, when problem solving seems more experimental, and some of our solutions may be true breakthroughs. This is when we are building and expanding the graphic vocabulary that will probably serve us the rest of our careers; when we are establishing our rules and parameters, and breaking them, and reestablishing them.

I've always felt that a design career was like a long, surreal staircase. At the bottom the risers are steep and the landings are short. One makes long leaps of discovery at the bottom in a relatively short period of time; a step a year, or two, and sometimes even one great leap to the middle of the stairs. Then, suddenly, the risers become shallow and the landings lengthen. We trudge along the same endless plateau and the scenery doesn't change. The light becomes dim around us, but there are sudden flashes back in the distance from the bottom of the steps. We don't dare turn around to look because we might lose our footing. Worse yet, the flashes seem ominous, hostile, like a potential fire that could burn up the whole staircase.

If only we could scamper to the top with the ease that we loped to the middle. Instead, we take baby steps and mutter, "Too much style and no substance," because we learned that line from higher-ups when we were hot young flashes at the bottom.

Very often, when we look at the work of our great graphic designer institutions, we find that so much of their truly important, innovative work was produced over a relatively short period of time: five years, ten years, flashes in the pan. Then there seems to be a leveling. Maybe these institutions never made it to the top of the staircase, but were merely inching along some other plateau in the dark. Maybe there is no top, just shorter risers and longer plateaus that go on forever.

Plateaus are actually very comfortable because it takes less energy to move. The problem is the dark. Perhaps the solution is to step aside and allow a flash to trot by. With a little light from that torch we may find the next step.

PAULA SCHER Poster for the Public Theater's *Bring in 'da Noise, Bring in 'da Funk*, 1995. The look and feel of Scher's work for the Public Theater became synonymous with New York City.

KARL GERSTNER Packaging for Teddymat, a laundry detergent brand marketed by Coop, a large union of Swiss retail chains, 1964. Here the formal motif of waves and foam link the products, turning each package into a flexible modular unit within a larger design system. Gerstner created this packaging while a partner in the ad agency Gerstner and Kutter. The same year, he wrote the cult classic *Designing Programmes*.

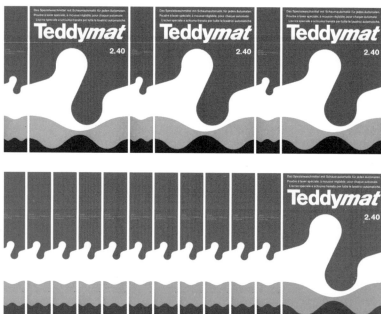

carl **schuricht**
maria **stader**
katharina **marti**
josef **traxel**
otto **von rohr**
beethoven
neunte sinfonie

juni-festwochen zürich
1957

tonhalle grosser saal
dienstag 2. juli 20.15 uhr
mittwoch 3. juli 20.15 uhr
1957
tonhallegesellschaft zürich
4. junifestkonzert   leitung carl schuricht
solisten
maria stader sopran
katharina marti alt
josef traxel tenor
otto von rohr bass
gemischter chor zürich
beethoven
neunte sinfonie in d-moll
op. 125

karten fr. 5.50 bis 16.50
tonhallekasse hug jecklin
kuoni

JOSEF MÜLLER-BROCKMANN
Junifestkonzert, one of a series
of posters developed for a
Zurich concert hall, the Tonhalle,
1957. Through these posters
Müller-Brockmann attempted
to communicate the music of
each particular concert using
an abstract modernist visual
language. This work exemplifies
the rigorous minimalist structure
of the International Style.

Modernism in America

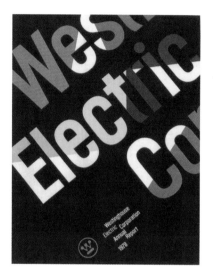

PAUL RAND Clockwise from top left: Westinghouse advertisement, 1962; IBM packaging, c. 1980; Cummins Engine annual report cover, 1979. These three layouts reflect some of Rand's best-known corporate design programs. American designers like Rand and Bauhaus immigrant Herbert Bayer used the almost scientific objectivity of Swiss design systems to position graphic design as a professional practice of value to corporate America. Such work pulled graphic design away from the more intuitive "big idea" approach of New York advertising of the 1950s and 1960s.

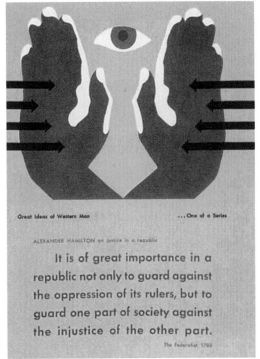

Great Ideas of Western Man   ...One of a Series

ALEXANDER HAMILTON on justice in a republic

It is of great importance in a
republic not only to guard against
the oppression of its rulers, but to
guard one part of society against
the injustice of the other part.

The Federalist, 1788

HERBERT BAYER Advertisement
for Noreen hair color, c. 1950-1955.
After immigrating to the United
States in 1938, Bayer took on
numerous independent commis-
sions including ads for Noreen.
Bayer, like Rand, understood that
the key to inventive work lay in
finding sophisticated corporate
sponsors with whom to partner.

HERBERT BAYER "Great Ideas
of Western Man" advertisement
commissioned by Walter Paepcke
for Container Corporation of
America, 1954.

This brilliant campaign is an early
example of branding. The product
itself, cardboard boxes, has little
to do with the ad concept. Each ad
in the series employed a different
famous quote and, led by Bayer,
often utilized the talents of famous
designers of the day, including
Paul Rand, Alvin Lustig, and György
Kepes. Bayer's long relationship
with CCA exemplifies the close ties
between business and design in the
United States during this period.

New Wave and Postmodernism

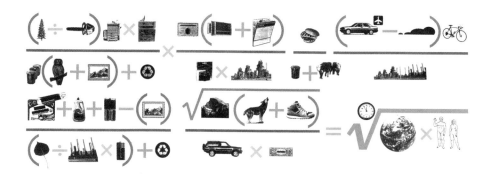

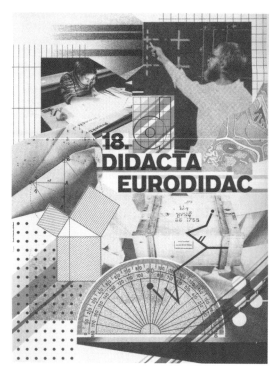

above: **KATHERINE MCCOY**
This design, titled "Renewal Equation," appeared in a booklet on the topic of recycling, recycled paper and environmental sustainability, to introduce Strathmore's recycled paper, 1990. This hypothetical "equation" speaks about the complexity of determining the environmental impacts of our megaconsumptive lives on planet Earth. All the images were copied from newspaper advertising supplements, using the trash of our commercial throwaway culture.

left: **WOLFGANG WEINGART**
Poster for the eighteenth Didacta/ Eurodidac at the Mustermesse convention center, 1981. Weingart led a second wave or "New Wave" of Swiss-style typography beginning in the 1960s. He explains in his autobiography, *My Way to Typography,* "I was motivated to provoke this stodgy profession and to stretch the type shop's capabilities to the breaking point and, finally, to prove once again that typography is an art."[1]

1 Wolfgang Weingart, *My Way to Typography,* trans. Katharine Wolff and Catherine Schelbert (Baden: Lars Müller, 2000), 112.

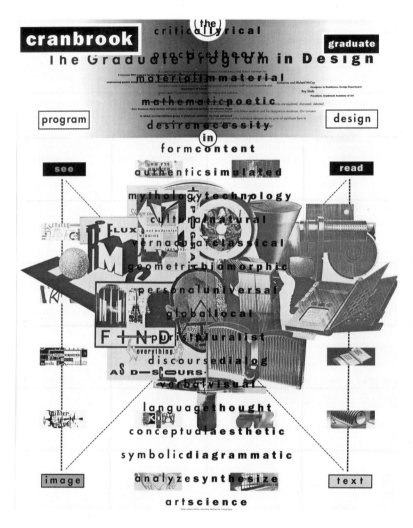

KATHERINE MCCOY Cranbrook Graduate Design "See Read" Poster, 1989. A photographic collage of recent graduate student work is overlaid by a list of possibly opposing design values and a diagram of communication theories. McCoy developed the "See Read" framework circa 1988 to model how deconstruction and structuralist/poststructuralist literary theories might be applied to graphic design's visual and verbal processes. The underlying premise is that a viewer receives stimuli in two modes: seeing—a visual, simultaneous, intuitive, experiential, perceptual, gestalt process; and reading—a verbal, sequential, learned, cerebral, decoding process. Typically we assume that viewers "see" images and "read" words, but this model also links "seeing" with text and "reading" with imagery.

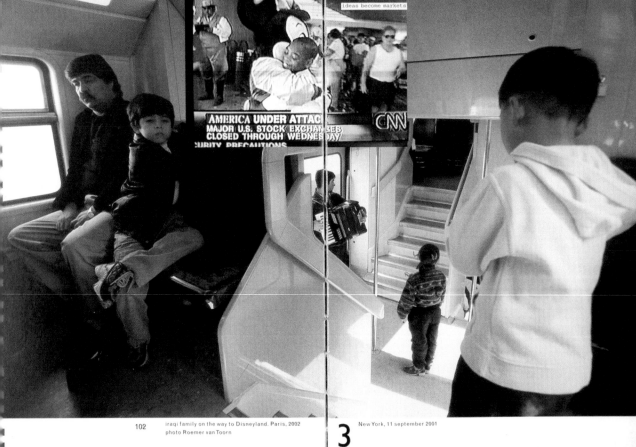

AMERICA UNDER ATTAC
MAJOR U.S. STOCK EXCHANGES
CLOSED THROUGH WEDNESDAY
URITY PRECAUTIONS

CNN

102   iraqi family on the way to Disneyland. Paris, 2002
photo Roemer van Toorn

3   New York, 11 september 2001

MAPPING THE FUTURE

AS ONE MILLENNIUM ENDED AND ANOTHER BEGAN, DIGITAL TECHNOLOGY FUNDAMENTALLY TRANSFORMED GRAPHIC DESIGN. OLD AVANT-GARDE ISSUES OF AUTHORSHIP, UNIVERSALITY, AND SOCIAL RESPONSIBILITY WERE REBORN WITHIN SOCIETY'S NEWLY DECENTRALIZED NETWORKED STRUCTURE. Designers became graphic authors, initiators of content, much to the chagrin of die-hard modernists and service-oriented professionals. Industry-standard software and restrictive web protocols formed a new universal graphic language, while the subjective shift expressed in New Wave and postmodern design instilled a revived sense of agency among designers. Kalle Lasn launched *Adbusters,* tearing a hole in the detached professional facade of the ad industry. Designers rebelled against the sleekness of technology, looking to a renewed sense of craft, as ornament reentered the design scene. Visionary global design leaders like Kenya Hara brought global consciousness and environmental ethos to big business. Cyber-space no longer represented the terrain of specialized interactive designers; instead virtual and physical reality began to merge, forming a new collective working environment for all.

JAN VAN TOORN Spread from the visual essay "Panorama of Habits" in *Design's Delight,* 2006.

STEVEN HELLER IS THE WORLD'S MOST PROLIFIC DESIGN WRITER, PRODUCING, SO FAR, OVER ONE HUNDRED BOOKS AND COUNTLESS ARTICLES. And, for the majority of his career, he has done so while maintaining a day job as an influential art director at the *New York Times* (first of the Op-Ed page and later of the Book Review). Notoriously, he begins his workday at 4:00 a.m. Since the late 1970s, Heller has filled such early morning hours documenting and critiquing the history and culture of graphic design, capturing narratives otherwise lost. As an educator he cofounded and cochairs the School of Visual Art's Designer as Author MFA program, and in 2008 he founded SVA's Design Criticism MFA. Heller speaks with a recognizable, strongly principled, sometimes controversial voice. Currently he is exploring the shifting terrain of blogs as both an editor and writer for online journals. In the entry below from Design Observer, Heller takes a sharp look at the advertising industry as he delves into the complex relationship between underground and mainstream design.

THE UNDERGROUND MAINSTREAM

STEVEN HELLER | 2008

Commercial culture depends on the theft of intellectual property for its livelihood. Mass marketers steal ideas from visionaries, alter them slightly if at all, then reissue them to the public as new products. In the process what was once insurgent becomes commodity, and what was once the shock of the new becomes the schlock of the novel. Invariably, early expressions of sub- or alternative cultures are the most fertile sampling grounds, as their publications or zines are the first to be pilfered. Invariably pioneers of radical form become wellsprings for appropriation. Rebellion of any kind breeds followers, and many followers become a demographic.

The phenomenon is not new, however. From the beginning of the twentieth century avant-gardes have ceded original ideas to the mass marketplace. In Europe the Weiner Werkstätte, Deutscher Werkbund, Bauhaus, and scores of other reformist schools and movements that sought to better the marketplace with convention-altering arts and crafts fell victim to their own successes. Their collective goal was to raise the level of both manufacture and design while changing timeworn habits and antiquated expectations, yet their ideas became established. The avant-garde is usurped when its eccentricity is deemed acceptable.

HOW CAN ONE DESIGN IF THE PAST IS UNKNOWN? AS A POLITICAL
TOOL IT HELPS TO UNDERSTAND THE LANGUAGE OF PERSUASION,
EVEN IF THE GOAL OF THE DESIGN BRIEF IS NOT TO CHANGE POLITICS.

STEVEN HELLER
"Graphics.com
Interview:
Steven Heller"
graphics.com
2007

In the 1920s Earnest Elmo Calkins, a progressive American advertising executive, argued that quotidian products and advertising campaigns must borrow characteristics from avant-garde European Modern art. Despite the avant-garde's antiestablishment symbolism, cubistic, futuristic, and expressionistic veneers, he argued, would capture the consumer's attention better than a hundred slogans. In the post–World War I era, when renewal was touted, new-and-improved-ness was the commercial mantra. But why waste time, Calkins reasoned, inventing something entirely new when the most experimental artists and designers of the age were already testing the tolerance of new ideas on their own dime. Calkins commanded commercial artists to appropriate and smooth out the edges of modern art, add an ornament here and there to make it palatable for the consumer class, and—voila!—instant allure and immediate sales.

He further proposed the doctrine of forced obsolescence to keep the traffic in new products moving. Calkins alleged that frequent cosmetic changes to everything from a soap package to a radio receiver cabinet would encourage consumers to discard the old, purchase the new, and replenish the economy. Waste was not an issue. Of course, this required true visionaries, skillful acolytes, and capable mimics. Commercial artists were indeed in the knock-off trade.

Yet when intrepid commercial artists attempted to push the boundaries of design, they had to be cognizant of what industrial designer Raymond Loewy called MAYA (Most Advanced Yet Acceptable). Fervent avant-gardists created truly unprecedented forms, but when they are commercialized a kind of trickle-down occurs. Invariably what begins as an elitist subculture follows a predictable trajectory from popular rejection to mass embrace.

Take the sixties psychedelic movement, for example: It was born in a small community that shared proclivities for sex, drugs, and anarchic behavior— all threatening to the mainstream. Kindred visual artists, musicians, and designers developed means of expression that helped define the culture's distinct characteristics. Psychedelic art was a distinct vocabulary, influenced by earlier graphic idioms, that overturned the rigid rules of clarity and legibility put forth by the once avant-garde moderns. Through its very raunchiness it manifested the ideals of the youth culture. For a brief time it was decidedly a shock to the system. But as it gained in popularity (like when it appeared on the cover of Hearst's Eye magazine or the sets of NBC's Laugh-In) it turned into a code easily co-opted by marketers.

Synthetic psychedelia was manufactured when the visions of the originators were co-opted by the profit motives of entrepreneurs. And what began as a pact of mutual self-interest turned into acts of cultural imperialism.

CRITICISM IS IMPORTANT BECAUSE IT GIVES US A LANGUAGE
(INDEED A LENS) BY WHICH TO DISCUSS AND VIEW DESIGN.

STEVEN HELLER
"The TH Interview:
A Quick Chat with
Steven Heller"
treehugger.com
2007

Underground bands led the way in a commercial whirlpool. They were given record contracts by labels owned by major corporations who wanted significant market share. In turn, the record labels advertised and packaged these bands using the very codes that signaled "alternative" to the growing youth market. Psychedelic design was this code. At first the look was fairly consistent with the original vision and motivation of the avant-garde pioneers. Many album covers of the period are today "classic" examples of true psyche-delic design. But within a very short period, as profits began to roll in, youth culture trend-spotters expanded the range, thereby dulling the edge, of the psychedelic style. Psychedelia was no longer an alternative code, it was the confirmation of conformist behavior, a uniform of alienation. The establish-ment still disapproved of the aesthetics, but it was difficult to be terrified of something that had become so integrated into the mass marketplace. Drugs were still bad, but psychedelia was just decorative. The avant-garde was commodified and the result was a mediocre, self-conscious rip-off. A hollow style that denoted an era remained.

During the ensuing decades the emergence of other confrontational art and design movements, including punk and grunge, that sought to unhinge dominant methods and mannerisms were ultimately absorbed into the mass culture. It has become axiomatic that fringe art, if it presumes to have any influence, will gravitate to, or be pushed towards, the center. All it takes is the followers of followers to cut a clear path to the mainstream. Indeed the main-stream embraces almost anything "edgy," although once the label is applied it is no longer on the edge.

Very little emerging from the underground fails to turn up in the mainstream. Pornography, once the bane of puritan society, is used by the advertising industry for edgy allure. Despite the occasional salvos by morality-in-media groups, all manner of publicly taboo sexuality appears in magazines and on billboards. Popular tolerances have increased to a level where shock in any realm is hard to come by.

Conversely, even before the mainstream began leeching off alternative cultures, the underground satirically appropriated from the mainstream. Today it's called "culture jamming," but in the twenties modern avant-gardists usurped the fundamental forms of commercial advertising by making art itself into advertising. What were Dada, futurist, and constructivist master-works if not advertisements for their new ideas? In promoting themselves they further expanded the visual languages of edgy advertising, which, not coincidentally, was later adopted by mainstream advertising.

Advertising has been a favored target for social critics. In the 1930s
Ballyhoo, a popular newsstand humor magazine (and the prototype for
Mad magazine, which in turn was the father of the sixties undergrounds
and the granddaddy of contemporary zines) savagely ripped the facade off
the hucksters on Madison Avenue. *Ballyhoo* took original quotidian ads for
automobiles, detergent, processed foods, you name it, wittily altered the
brand-names (à la *Adbusters*) and caricatured the product pitches to reveal
the inherent absurdities in the product claims. Likewise, in the fifties and
early sixties *Mad* magazine skewered major brands by attacking the insidious
slogans endemic to advertising. They issued such classics as "Look Ma, No
Cavities, and No Teeth Either," a send-up of Crest Toothpaste's false promise
of cavity-free teeth, and "Happy But Wiser," a slam at Budweiser beer through
a parody ad that showed a besotted, forlorn alcoholic whose wife had just
dumped him. *Mad* was the influence for Wacky Packages (created by Art
Spiegelman), which came inside Topps bubble gum packages and used puns
on mainstream product brand-names to attack society, politics, and culture
(i.e., Reaganets, a takeoff on the candy Raisinets that looked like the former
American president). Paradoxically, *Ballyhoo*, *Mad*, and Wacky Packages were
all mass-market products, but because of their respective exposure each had an
influence on the kids who grew up to produce the icons of alternative culture.

Underground denizens attack the mainstream for two reasons: To alter
or to join, sometimes both. Few designers choose to be outsiders forever.
Outsiders are, after all, invariably marginalized until the mainstream celebrates them as unsung geniuses. Outsiders may choose to join the mainstream
on their own terms, but join they must to be able to make an impact larger
than their circumscribed circles. This is perhaps one reason why so many
self-described rebels enter mainstream advertising, and now viral advertising.
"It's where the best resources are," one young creative director for a "progressive" New York firm told me. "It's also where I believe that I can make the most
impact on the future of the medium and maybe even culture." In fact, on the
wall of his office hangs a sheet of yellowing old Wacky Package stickers. "This
is advertising at its best," he explains. "Because it is ironic, self-flagellating,
and irreverent. The best advertising should be done with wit and humor, with
a wink and nod. Self parody is the thing." Indeed the process has come full
circle. Today, designers for mainstream advertising companies, weaned on
alternative approaches, have folded the underground into the mainstream
and call it "cool."

This blog entry on Design Observer incited many comments. Visit designobserver.com to read the additional commentary.

JAN VAN TOORN REVEALS THE DESIGNER BEHIND THE DESIGN, THE IDEOLOGY BEHIND THE AESTHETICS. Since the 1960s, he has used his design work to unveil the social and cultural implications of mass media. Using physical acts of cut-and-paste, he often combines media imagery into new statements. Through his theoretical books and his commercial work he emphasizes to us that visual communication is never neutral, the designer never simply an objective conveyer of information. Van Toorn is critical, political, and, in some cases, polarizing. As an educator at universities and academies in the Netherlands and abroad, including the Rhode Island School of Design, van Toorn urges his students to take responsibility for their own role within the ideology of our culture. Born in 1932, this influential Dutch graphic and exhibition designer warns us that design has "become imprisoned in a fiction that does not respond to factual reality." The essay below urges designers to engage and expose the established symbolic order.

DESIGN AND REFLEXIVITY

JAN VAN TOORN | 1994

LE PAIN ET LA LIBERTÉ

Every professional practice operates in a state of schizophrenia, in a situation full of inescapable contradictions. So too communicative design, which traditionally views its own action as serving the public interest, but which is engaged at the same time in the private interests of clients and media. To secure its existence, design, like other practical intellectual professions, must constantly strive to neutralize these inherent conflicts of interest by developing a mediating concept aimed at consensus. This always comes down to a reconciliation with the present state of social relations; in other words, to accepting the world image of the established order as the context for its own action.

By continually smoothing over the conflicts in the production relationships, design, in cooperation with other disciplines, has developed a practical and conceptual coherence that has afforded it representational and institutional power in the mass media. In this manner it legitimizes itself in the eyes of the established social order, which, in turn, is confirmed and legitimized by the contributions that design makes to symbolic production. It is this image of reality, in particular of the social world that, pressured by the market economy, no longer has room for emancipatory engagement as a foundation for critical practice.

Design has thus become imprisoned in a fiction that does not respond to factual reality beyond the representations of the culture industry and its communicative monopoly. In principle, this intellectual impotence is still expressed in dualistic, product-oriented action and thought: on the one hand there is the individual's attempt to renew the vocabulary—out of resistance to the social integration of the profession; on the other there is the intention to arrive at universal and utilitarian soberness of expression—within the existing symbolic and institutional order. Although the lines separating these two extremes are becoming blurred (as a consequence of postmodernist thinking and ongoing market differentiation), official design continues to be characterized by aesthetic compulsiveness and/or by a patriarchal fixation on reproductive ordering.

The social orientation of our action as designers is no longer as simple as that. We seem happy enough to earn our living in blind freedom, leading to vulgarization and simplification of our reflective and critical traditions. That is why it is time to apply our imaginative power once again to how we deal with communicative reality.

The intermediary lays down the law. Mediation determines the nature of the message, there is a primacy of the relation over being. In other words, it is the bodies that think, not the minds. The constraint of incorporation produces corporations, which are these intermediary bodies and these institutions of knowledge, abided by norms and formulating norms, known as schools, churches, parties, associations, debating societies, etc.
Régis Debray | *Media Manifestos: On the Technological Transmission of Cultural Forms* | 1996

The given facts that appear…as the positive index of truth are in fact the negation of truth….Truth can only be established by their destruction.
Herbert Marcuse | *Reason and Revolution: Hegel and the Rise of Social Theory* | 1941

Valid critical judgment is the fruit not of spiritual dissociation but of an energetic collusion with everyday life.
Terry Eagleton | *The Function of Criticism: From the Spectator to Post-Structuralism* | 1985

Criticism is not an innocent discipline, and has never been….The moment when a material or intellectual practice begins to "think itself," to take itself as an object of intellectual inquiry, is clearly of dominant significance in the development of that practice; it will certainly never be the same again. What thrusts such a practice into self-reflexiveness is not merely an internal pressure, but the complex unity it forms with adjacent discourses.
Terry Eagleton | *Criticism and Ideology: A Study in Marxist Literary Theory* | 1976

SYMBOLIC FORMS ARE SOCIAL FORMS

Symbolic productions represent the social position and mentality of the elites that create and disseminate them. As ideological instruments, they serve private interests that are preferably presented as universal ones. The dominant culture does not serve to integrate the ruling classes only, however; "It also contributes," as Pierre Bourdieu describes it, "to the fictitious integration of society as a whole, and thus to the apathy (false consciousness) of the dominated classes; and finally, it contributes to the legitimation of the established order by establishing distinctions (hierarchies) and legitimating these distinctions."[1] Consequently, the dominant culture forces all

1 Pierre Bourdieu, *Language and Symbolic Power* (Cambridge, MA: Harvard University Press, 1991), 167.

other cultures to define themselves in its symbolism, this being the instrument of knowledge and communication. This communicative dependency is particularly evident in the "solutions" that the dominant culture proposes for the social, economic, and political problems of what is defined as the "periphery"—of those who do not (yet) belong.

By definition, the confrontation between reality and symbolic representation is uncertain. This uncertainty has now become undoubtedly painful, since, as Jean Baudrillard puts it, the experience of reality has disappeared "behind the mediating hyperreality of the simulacrum." A progressive staging of everyday life that gives rise to great tension between ethics and symbolism, because of the dissonance between the moral intentions related to reality and the generalizations and distinctions of established cultural production.

For an independent and oppositional cultural production, another conceptual space must be created that lies beyond the destruction of direct experience by the simulacrum of institutional culture. The point is not to create a specific alternative in the form of a new dogma as opposed to the spiritual space of the institutions. On the contrary, the point is to arrive at a "mental ecology"[2] that makes it possible for mediating intellectuals, like designers, to leave the beaten path, to organize their opposition, and to articulate that in the mediated display. This is only possible by adopting a radically different position with respect to the production relationships—by exposing the variety of interests and disciplinary edifices in the message, commented on and held together by the mediator's "plane of consistency."[3]

2 Félix Guattari, "Postmodernism and Ethical Abdications," *Profile* 39 (1993): 11-13.

3 Gilles Deleuze and Félix Guattari, *A Thousand Plateaus* (Minneapolis: University of Minnesota Press, 1987), 506-508.

Symbolic power does not reside in "symbolic systems" in the form of an "illocutionary force" but…is defined in and through a given relation between those who exercise power and those who submit to it, i.e., in the very structure of the field in which belief is produced and reproduced.
Pierre Bourdieu | *Social Theory for a Changing Society* | 1991

Designers must come to reflect upon the functions they serve, and on the potentially hazardous implications of those functions. In the 1930s, Walter Benjamin wrote that humankind's "self-alienation has reached such a degree that it can experience its own destruction as an aesthetic pleasure of the first order."
Stuart Ewen | "Notes for the New Millennium" | *ID* 31, no. 2 | March-April 1990

AND MEDIOCRITY

Opportunities for renewed engagement must be sought in initiatives creating new public polarities, according to Félix Guattari, in "untying the bonds of language" and "[opening] up new social, analytical, and aesthetic practices."[4] This will only come about within the context of a political approach that, unlike the dominant neoliberal form of capitalism, is directed at real social problems. If we are to break through the existing communicative order, this "outside thought"[5] should also reverberate in the way in which designers interpret the theme and program of the client. In

4 Guattari, "Postmodernism."

5 Michel Foucault, "Maurice Blanchot: The Thought from Outside," in *Foucault/Blanchot*, trans. Jeffrey Mehiman and Brian Massumi (New York: Zone Books, 1987).

other words, the designer must take on an oppositional stance, implying a departure from the circle of common-sense cultural representation. This is an important notion, because the point is no longer to question whether the message is true, but whether it works as an argument—one that manifests itself more or less explicitly in the message, in relation to the conditions under which it was produced and under which it is disseminated.

Such activity is based on a multidimensional, complementary way of thinking with an essentially different attitude to viewers and readers. It imposes a complementary structure on the work as well, an assemblage that is expressed both in content and in form. The essence of this approach, however, is that, through the critical orientation of its products, the reflexive mentality raises questions among the public that stimulate a more active way of dealing with reality. In this manner it may contribute to a process that allows us to formulate our own needs, interest, and desires and resist the fascination with the endless fragmented and aestheticized varieties created by the corporate culture of commerce, state, media, and "attendant" disciplines.

The arts of imitation need something wild, primitive, striking....
First of all move me, surprise me...make me tremble, weep, shudder, outrage me; delight my eyes afterwards if you can.
Denis Diderot | "Essai sur la peinture" | 1766

The more it becomes clear that architecture is a total impossibility today, the more exciting I find it. I have a great aversion to architecture in the classical sense, but now that this kind of architecture has become entirely impossible, I am excited to involve myself in it again....It is indeed schizophrenic. Our work is a battle against architecture in the form of architecture.
Rem Koolhaas | De Architect 25 | 1994.

For the situation, Brecht says, is complicated by the fact that less than ever does a simple reproduction of reality express something about reality. A photograph of the Krupp works or the A.E.G. reveals almost nothing about these institutions. The real reality has shifted over to the functional. The reification of human relations, for instance in industry, makes the latter no longer revealing. Thus in fact it is to build something up, some-thing artistic, created.
Walter Benjamin | "A Short History of Photography" | 1880

Not surprisingly, institutions and galleries are often resistant to products that question generally held opinions and tastes....But the peculiar dialectics of consciousness,...and given the relative lack of uniformity of interests within the culture industry and among its consumers, nevertheless promote the surfacing of such critical works....With this modicum of openness, wherever suitable, the [galleries'] promotional resources should be used without hesitation for a critique of the dominant system of beliefs while employing the very mechanisms of that system.
Hans Haacke | Radical Attitudes to the Gallery | 1977

There are two positions in the mass media. The first says that if something works, it is correct....This idea is the enemy of our concept. On the other hand, you have a principle of authenticity. Enlightened narration accepts authenticity. I do not continually try to make general concepts that control the individual; rather I let something retain its own genuineness....There follows from this a number of organizational principles....In the structuring of a particular work, that is, inaesthetic method.
Alexander Kluge | "On New German Cinema, Art, Enlightenment, and the Public Sphere: An Interview with Alexander Kluge" | 1988

SUBVERSIVE PLEASURES

Despite the symbolically indeterminable nature of culture, communicative design, as reflexive practice, must be realistic in its social ambitions. In the midst of a multiplicity of factors too numerous to take stock of, all of which influence the product, the aim is to arrive at a working method that produces commentaries rather than confirms self-referential fictions. Design will have to get used to viewing substance, program, and style as ideological constructions, as expressions of restricted choices that only show a small sliver of reality in mediation. The inevitable consequence is that the formulation of messages continues to refer to the fundamental uneasiness between symbolic infinity and the real world.

This mentality demands a major investment in practical discourse in those fields and situations where experience and insight can be acquired through work. This is important not only because it is necessary to struggle against design in the form of design, echoing Rem Koolhaas's statement about architecture, but also because partners are required with the same operational options.[6] It is furthermore of public interest to acquaint a wider audience with forms of communication contributing to more independent and radical democratic shaping of opinion.

Moving from a reproductive order to a commentating one, operative criticism can make use of a long reflexive practice. All cultures have communicative forms of fiction that refer to their own fictitiousness in resistance to the established symbolic order. "To this end," Robert Stam writes, "they deploy myriad strategies—narrative discontinuities, authorial intrusions, essayistic digressions, stylistic virtuosities. They share a playful, parodic, and disruptive relation to established norms and conventions. They demystify fictions, and our naive faith in fictions, and make of this demystification a source for new fictions!"[7] This behavior alone constitutes a continuous "ecological" process for qualitative survival in social and natural reality.

6 Rem Koolhaas, "De ontplooiing van de architectuur," *De Architect* 25 (The Hague: ten Hagen en Stam, 1994): 16-25.

7 Robert Stam, *Reflexivity in Film and Literature: From Don Quixote to Jean-Luc Godard* (New York: Columbia University Press, 1992), xi.

The control of representation and definition remains concentrated in the products and services of media-cultural combines. That control can be challenged and lessened only by political means.... Theories that ignore the structure and locus of representational and definitional power and emphasize instead the individual's message of transformational capability present little threat to the maintenance of the established order.
Herbert Schiller | *Culture Inc: The Corporate Takeover of Public Expression* | 1989

Survival in fact is about the connections between things; in Eliot's phrase, reality cannot be deprived of the "other echoes [that] inhabit the garden." It is more rewarding—and more difficult—to think concretely and sympathetically, contrapuntally, about others than only about "us."
Edward Said | *Culture and Imperialism* | 1993

My goal is to raise a critical attitude, raise questions about reality, curiosity.
Gérard Paris-Clavel | in a conversation with van Toorn | Paris, 1994

The challenge for anti-illusionist fictions is how to respect the fabulating impulse, how to revel in the joys of storytelling and the delights of artifice, while maintaining a certain intellectual distance from the story. The subversive pleasure generated by a Cervantes, a Brecht, or a Godard consists in telling stories while comically undermining their authority. The enemy to do away with, after all, is not fiction but socially generated illusion; not stories but alienated dreams.
Robert Stam | *Reflexivity in Film and Literature: From Don Quixote to Jean-Luc Godard* | 1992

**"WHAT DESIGN NEEDS," KALLE LASN PROCLAIMS, "IS TEN YEARS OF TOTAL TURMOIL...
ANARCHY...AFTER THAT MAYBE IT WILL MEAN SOMETHING AGAIN...STAND FOR SOMETHING
AGAIN."** He warns graphic designers, "We have lost our plot. Our story line. We have lost our soul."[1] *Design
Anarchy*, excerpted below, is his sprawling manifesto. Through it, Lasn forces us to look straight at the harmful
consequences of our profession. He rolls out the psychological and environmental damage of overconsump-
tion. Designers, he challenges, created a crisis—and they can solve it. Born in Estonia during World War II, Lasn
lived in a displaced person's camp as a young boy. Later he moved with his family to Australia, then spent his
early adulthood traveling the world. In 1989 Lasn founded the Canadian-based magazine *Adbusters.* Through
Adbusters and the larger "culture jamming" movement, this marketing man turned media activist fights media
with media.[2] Graphic design, he reminds us, is a powerful profession that can have nasty societal consequences.

1   Kalle Lasn, "The Future of Design"
    (lecture, TYPO Berlin, 11th
    International Design Conference,
    Berlin, May 2006).

2   For more information about culture
    jamming, see www.adbusters.org.

DESIGN ANARCHY

KALLE LASN | 2006

CULTURAL REVOLUTION IS OUR BUSINESS

We are a global network of artists, writers, environmentalists, teachers,
downshifters, fair traders, rabble-rousers, shit-disturbers, incorrigibles, and
malcontents. We are anarchists, guerrilla tacticians, meme warriors, neo-
Luddites, pranksters, poets, philosophers, and punks. Our aim is to topple
existing power structures and change the way we live in the twenty-first
century. We will change the way information flows, the way institutions wield
power, the way the food, fashion, car, and culture industries set their agendas.
Above all, we will change the way we interact with the mass media and the
way in which meaning is produced in our society.

DESIGN ANARCHY

Design Anarchy is madness. Choose it only if you're certain the other options
will corrode your soul and give you a bleeding ulcer, only if you know you
are among the chosen few designers who hold Prometheus's holy fire in your
hands. You'll suffer for years and live like a stray dog, but you'll have the joy of
breaking all the rules, of freely mixing art and politics, of pouring your beliefs
and convictions into your work. Eventually, if you're really as brilliant as you
think, you'll have a crack at pushing the boundaries of global culture with bold
new forms and fresh ways of being.

MICHAEL ROCK STRADDLES TWO WORLDS: ONE ACADEMIC, ONE PRACTICAL. In the 1980s and early 1990s, first at the Rhode Island School of Design and later at Yale University, Rock rallied the profession to embrace design criticism. And he led with his own writings. His seminal 1996 text, "The Designer as Author," provoked a debate—which still rages today—over the authorship of design content. In it Rock poses the question: "What does it really mean to call for a graphic designer to be an author?" At the height of his academic success, he jumped from the ivory tower and into the commercial world, taking a gang of colleagues with him to become, in his words, "makers instead of critics."[1] They founded 2x4, a professional design practice known for high-level collaborative work for clients like Prada. Today, his work is considered conceptual, thought provoking, and highly process driven. From Yale to Prada, from critic to maker, Rock's journey emphasizes the importance of theory to our field. His carefully considered essay gives shape and depth to this larger debate, just as his abstract intellectual approach to practical, professional work gives shape and depth to his designs.

1 Michael Rock, An AIA SF/SFMOMA public lecture and podcast video program. San Francisco: Architecture Radio, September 9, 2005, http://www.architecture-radio.org/learn/public/20050922-ROCK (accessed July 9, 2008).

THE DESIGNER AS AUTHOR

MICHAEL ROCK | 1996

Graphic authorship may be an idea whose time has come, but it is not without its contradictions.

"Authorship" has become a popular term in graphic design circles, especially in those at the edges of the profession: the design academies and the murky territory between design and art. The word has an important ring to it, with seductive connotations of origination and agency. But the question of how designers become authors is a difficult one, and exactly who qualifies and what authored design might look like depends on how you define the term and determine admission into the pantheon.

Authorship may suggest new approaches to the issue of the design process in a profession traditionally associated more with the communication rather than the origination of messages. But theories of authorship also serve as legitimizing strategies, and authorial aspirations may end up reinforcing certain conservative notions of design production and subjectivity—ideas that run counter to recent critical attempts to overthrow the perception of design as based on individual brilliance. The implications of such a re-definition deserve careful scrutiny. What does it really mean to call for a graphic designer to be an author?

The meaning of the word "author" has shifted significantly through history and has been the subject of intense scrutiny over the last forty years. The earliest definitions are not associated with writing per se, but rather denote "the person who originates or gives existence to anything." Other usages have authoritarian—even patriarchal—connotations: "the father of all life," "any inventor, constructor or founder," "one who begets," and "a director, commander, or ruler." More recently, Wimsatt and Beardsley's seminal essay "The Intention Fallacy" (1946) was one of the first to drive a wedge between the author and the text with its claim that a reader could never really "know" the author through his or her writing.[2] The so-called "Death of the Author," proposed most succinctly by Roland Barthes in a 1968 essay of that name, is closely linked to the birth of critical theory, especially theory based in reader response and interpretation rather than intentionality.[3] Michel Foucault used the rhetorical question "What Is an Author?" in 1969 as the title of an influential essay that, in response to Barthes, outlines the basic characteristics and functions of the author and the problems associated with conventional ideas of authorship and origination.[4]

Foucault demonstrated that over the centuries the relationship between the author and the text has changed. The earliest sacred texts are authorless, their origins lost in history. In fact, the ancient, anonymous origin of such texts serves as a kind of authentication. On the other hand, scientific texts, at least until after the Renaissance, demanded an author's name as validation. By the eighteenth century, however, Foucault asserts, the situation had reversed: literature was authored and science had become the product of anonymous objectivity. Once authors began to be punished for their writing—that is, when a text could be transgressive—the link between the author and the text was firmly established. Text became a kind of private property, owned by the author, and a critical theory developed that reinforced that relationship, searching for keys to the text in the life and intention of its writer. With the rise of scientific method, on the other hand, scientific texts and mathematical proofs were no longer seen as authored texts but as discovered truths. The scientist revealed an extant phenomenon, a fact anyone faced with the same conditions would have uncovered. Therefore the scientist and mathematician could be the first to discover a paradigm, and lend their name to it, but could never claim authorship over it.

Poststructuralist readings tend to criticize the prestige attributed to the figure of the author. The focus shifts from the author's intention to the internal workings of the writing: not what it means but how it means. Barthes ends his essay supposing "the birth of the reader must be at the cost of the death of the Author."[5] Foucault imagines a time when we might ask, "What difference does it make who is speaking?"[6] The notion that a text is a line of words that releases a single meaning, the central message of an author/god, is overthrown.

2 W. K. Wimsatt and Monroe C. Beardsley, "The Intentional Fallacy," in Hazard Adams, ed., *Critical Theory since Plato* (New York: Harcourt Brace Jovanovich, 1971), 1015-1022.

3 Roland Barthes, "The Death of the Author," in *Image-Music-Text*, trans. Stephen Heath (New York: Hill and Wang, 1977), 142-148.

4 Michel Foucault, "What Is an Author?" in Josué Harari, ed., *Textual Strategies* (Ithaca: Cornell University Press, 1979), 141-160.

5 Barthes, "The Death," 145.

6 Foucault, "What Is an Author?" 160.

7 Fredric Jameson, quoted in Mark Dery, "The Persistence of Industrial Memory," *Any* 10 (1995): 25.

8 Katherine McCoy, "The New Discourse," *Design Quarterly* 148 (1990): 16.

9 Barthes, "The Death," 146.

10 Ellen Lupton and J. Abbott Miller, "Deconstruction and Graphic Design: History Meets Theory," in "New Perspectives: Critical Histories of Graphic Design: Part 2," ed. Andrew Blauvelt, special issue, *Visible Language* 28, no. 2 (Autumn 1994): 352.

11 Paul de Man, "Semiology and Rhetoric," in *Harari, Textual Strategies,* 121.

12 Josef Müller-Brockmann, *Grid Systems in Graphic Design* (Stuttgart: Verlag Gerd Jatje, 1981), 10.

Postmodernism turned on a "fragmented and schizophrenic decentering and dispersion" of the subject, noted Fredric Jameson.[7] The notion of a decentered text—a text that is skewed from the direct line of communication between sender and receiver, severed from the authority of its origin, and exists as a free-floating element in a field of possible significations—has figured heavily in recent constructions of a design based in reading and readers. But Katherine McCoy's prescient image of designers moving beyond problem-solving and by "authoring additional content and a self-conscious critique of the message…adopting roles associated with art and literature" has as often as not been misconstrued.[8] Rather than working to incorporate theory into their methods of production, many so-called "deconstructivist" designers literally illustrated Barthes's image of a reader-based text—"a tissue of quotations drawn from innumerable centers of culture"—by scattering fragments of quotations across the surface of their "authored" posters and book covers.[9] The dark implications of Barthes's theory, note Ellen Lupton and J. Abbott Miller, were fashioned into "a romantic theory of self expression."[10]

Perhaps after years as faceless facilitators, designers were ready to speak out. Some may have been eager to discard the internal affairs of formalism—to borrow a metaphor used by Paul de Man—and branch out into the foreign affairs of external politics and content.[11] By the 1970s design had begun to discard the scientific approach that had held sway for decades, exemplified by the rationalist ideology that preached strict adherence to an eternal grid.

Müller-Brockmann's evocation of the "aesthetic quality of mathematical thinking" is the clearest and most cited example of this approach.[12] Müller-Brockmann and a slew of fellow researchers such as Kepes, Dondis, and Arnheim worked to uncover a preexisting order and form in the way a scientist reveals "truth." But what is most peculiar and revealing in Müller-Brockmann's writing is his reliance on tropes of submission: the designer submits to the will of the system, forgoes personality, withholds interpretation.

On the surface, at least, it would seem that designers were moving away from authorless, scientific texts—in which inviolable visual principles arrived at through extensive visual research were revealed—towards a position in which the designer could claim some level of ownership over the message (and this at a time when literary theory was moving away from that very position). But some of the institutional features of design practice are at odds with zealous attempts at self-expression. The idea of a decentered message does not necessarily sit well in a professional relationship in which the client is paying the designer to convey specific information or emotions.

In addition, most design is done in a collaborative setting, either within a client relationship or in the context of a studio that utilizes the talents of numerous creative people, with the result that the origin of any particular idea is uncertain. The ever-present pressure of technology and electronic communication only muddies the water further.

IS THERE AN AUTEUR IN THE HOUSE?

It is perhaps not surprising that Barthes's "The Death of the Author" was written in Paris in 1968, the year students joined workers on the barricades in a general strike and the Western world flirted with real social revolution. The call for the overthrow of authority in the form of the author in favor of the reader—i.e., the masses—had a real resonance in 1968. But to lose power you must have already worn a mantle, which is perhaps why designers had a problem in trying to overthrow a power that they never possessed.

The figure of the author implied a totalitarian control over creative activity and seemed an essential ingredient of high art. If the relative level of genius—on the part of the author, painter, sculptor, or composer—was the ultimate measure of artistic achievement, activities that lacked a clear central authority figure were devalued. The development of film theory during the period serves as an interesting example. In 1954 film critic and budding film director François Truffaut had first promulgated the "politique des auteurs," a polemical strategy developed to reconfigure a critical theory of the cinema.[13] The problem was how to create a theory that imagined a film, necessarily the result of broad collaboration, as the work of a single artist, thus a work of art. The solution was to determine a set of criteria that allowed a critic to define certain directors as auteurs. In order to establish the film as a work of art, auteur theory held that the director—hitherto merely one-third of the creative troika of director, writer, and cinematographer—had ultimate control over the entire project.

Auteur theory—especially as espoused by the American critic Andrew Sarris—speculated that directors must meet three criteria in order to pass into the sacred hall of auteurs.[14] Sarris proposed that the director must demonstrate technical expertise, have a stylistic signature that is visible over the course of several films, and, through his or her choice of projects and cinematic treatment, show a consistency of vision and interior meaning. Since the film director had little control of the material he or she worked with—especially within the Hollywood studio system, where directors were assigned to projects—the signature way a range of scripts was treated was especially important.

13 Jim Hiller, *Cahiers du cinema: The 1950s: Neo-Realism, Hollywood, New Wave* (Cambridge, MA: Harvard University Press, 1985), 4.

14 Andrew Sarris, *The Primal Screen* (New York: Simon and Schuster, 1973), 50-51.

THE DIFFERENCE BETWEEN DESIGNERS IS REVEALED IN THE
UNIQUE WAY EACH INDIVIDUAL DESIGNER APPROACHES CONTENT,
NOT THE CONTENT THEY GENERATE.

MICHAEL ROCK
"Fuck Content"
2005

The interesting thing about auteur theory is that film theorists, like designers, had to construct the notion of the author as a means of raising what was considered low entertainment to the plateau of fine art. The parallels between film direction and design practice are striking. Like the film director, the art director or designer is often distanced from his or her material and works collaboratively on it, directing the activity of a number of other creative people. In addition, over the course of a career both the film director and the designer work on a number of different projects with varying levels of creative potential. As a result, any inner meaning must come from aesthetic treatment as much as from content.

If we apply the criteria used to identify auteurs to graphic designers, we yield a body of work that may be elevated to auteur status. Technical proficiency could be claimed by any number of practitioners, but couple this with a signature style and the field narrows. The designers who fulfill these criteria will be familiar to any *Eye* reader; many of them have been featured in the magazine. (And, of course, selective republishing of certain work and exclusion of other construct a stylistically consistent oeuvre.) The list would probably include Fabian Baron, Tibor Kalman, David Carson, Neville Brody, Edward Fella, Anthon Beeke, Pierre Bernard, Gert Dunbar, Tadanoori Yokoo, Vaughn Oliver, Rick Valicenti, April Greiman, Jan van Toorn, Wolfgang Weingart, and many others. But great technique and style alone do not an auteur make. If we add the requirement of interior meaning, how does this list fare? Are there designers who by special treatment and choice of projects approach the issue of deeper meaning in the way Bergman, Hitchcock, or Welles does?

How do you compare a film poster with the film itself? The very scale of a cinematic project allows for a sweep of vision not possible in graphic design. Therefore graphic auteurs, almost by definition, would have to have produced large established bodies of work in which discernible patterns emerge. Who, then, are the graphic auteurs? Perhaps Bernard and van Toorn, possibly Oliver, Beeke, and Fella. There is a sense of getting a bigger idea, a deeper quality to their work, aided in the case of Bernard and van Toorn by their political affiliations and in Oliver by long association that produces a consistent genre of music, allowing for a range of experimentation. In these cases the graphic auteur both seeks projects he is commissioned to work on from a specific, recognizable critical perspective. Van Toorn will look at a brief for a corporate annual report from a socioeconomic position; Bernard evokes a position of class struggle, capitalist brutality, and social dysfunction; and Oliver examines dark issues of decay, rapture, and the human body. Jean Renoir observed that an artistic director spends his whole career remaking variations on the same film.

Great stylists such as Carson and Baron do not seem to qualify for admission to the auteur pantheon, at least according to Sarris's criteria, as it is difficult to discern a message in their work that transcends the stylistic elegance of the typography in the case of Baron and the studied inelegance of that of Carson. (You have to ask yourself, "What is their work about?") Valicenti and Brody try to inject inner meaning into their work—as in Valicenti's self-published Aids advertising and Brody's attachment to the post-linguistic alphabet systems—but their output remains impervious to any such intrusion. A judgment such as this, however, brings us to the Achilles' heel of auteur theory. In trying to describe interior meaning, Sarris resorts to "the intangible difference between one personality and another."[15] That retreat to intangibility—the "I can't say what it is but I know it when I see it" aspect—is one of the reasons why the theory has long since fallen into disfavor in film criticism circles. It also never dealt adequately with the collaborative nature of cinema and the messy problems of movie-making. But while the theory is passé, its effect is still with us: the director to this day sits squarely at the center of our perception of film structure. In the same way, it could be that we have been applying a modified graphic auteur theory for years without being aware of it. After all, what is design theory if not a series of critical elevations and demotions as our attitudes about style, meaning, and significance evolve? [...]

FORWARD OR BACKWARD?

If the ways a designer can be an author are complex and confused, the way designers have used the term and the value ascribed to it are equally so. Any number of recent statements claim authorship as the panacea to the woes of the brow-beaten designer. A recent call for entries for a design exhibition entitled "Designer as Author: Voices and Visions" sought to identify "graphic designers who are engaged in work that transcends the traditional service-oriented commercial production, and who pursue projects that are personal, social, or investigative in nature."[16] The rejection of the role of the facilitator and call to "transcend" traditional production imply that the authored design holds some higher, purer purpose. The amplification of the personal voice legitimizes design as equal to more traditional privileged forms of authorship.

15 Andrew Sarris, "Notes on the Auteur Theory in 1962," in P. Adams Sitney, ed., *Film Culture Reader* (New York: Praeger Publishers, 1970), 133.

16 "Re:Quest for Submissions" to the "Designer as Author: Voices and Visions" exhibition, Northern Kentucky University, 1996.

But if designers should aim for open readings and free textual interpretations—as a litany of contemporary theorists have convinced us—that desire is thwarted by oppositional theories of authorship. Foucault noted that the figure of the author is not a particularly liberating one: the author as origin, authority, and ultimate owner of the text guards against the free will of the reader. Transferring the authority of the text back over to the author contains and categorizes the work, narrowing the possibilities for interpretation. The figure of the author reconfirms the traditional idea of the genius creator; the status of the creator frames the work and imbues it with mythical value.

While some claims for authorship may be simply an indication of a renewed sense of responsibility, at times they seem ploys to gain proper rights, attempts to exercise some kind of agency where there has traditionally been none. Ultimately the author equals authority. While the longing for graphic authorship may be the longing for legitimacy or power, is celebrating the design as central character necessarily a positive move? Isn't that what has fuelled the last fifty years of design history? If we really want to go beyond the designer-as-hero model, we may have to imagine a time when we can ask, "What difference does it make who designed it?"

On the other hand, work is created by someone. (All those calls for the death of the author are made by famous authors.) While the development and definition of artistic styles, and their identification and classification, are at the heart of an outmoded Modernist criticism, we must still work to engage these problems in new ways. It may be that the real challenge is to embrace the multiplicity of methods—artistic and commercial, individual and collaborative—that comprises design language. An examination of the designer-as-author could help us to rethink process, expand design methods, and elaborate our historical frame to incorporate all forms of graphic discourse. But while theories of graphic authorship may change the way work is made, the primary concern of both the viewer and the critic is not who made it, but rather what it does and how it does it.

DMITRI SIEGEL EPITOMIZES THE NEW GENERATION OF DESIGN THINKERS. He is a pragmatic intellectual who approaches crucial graphic design issues from the working field. While contributing essays regularly to the influential blog Design Observer, as well as myriad other publications, Siegel is the creative director for interactive and video for Urban Outfitters, a partner in the publicity venture Ante Projects, and creative director for the magazine *Anathema*. He is also on the faculty of the Art Center College of Design and has taught at University of the Arts in Philadelphia. Siegel stands solidly on the "sliver of land suspended between culture and commerce," a situation he once described as "the defining characteristic of graphic design."[1] In the Design Observer entry printed below, he takes on the emerging cultural and economic model of consumer as producer. Siegel describes this new DIY style of consumerism as "prosumerism—simultaneous production and consumption." Where, he asks, does the graphic designer fit within the new model? Who do we work for, if everyone is "designing-it-themselves"?

1 Dmitri Siegel, "Context in Cri-
tique (review of *Émigré* No. 64,
Rant)," *Adbusters* (September–
October 2003): 79–81.

DESIGNING OUR OWN GRAVES

DMITRI SIEGEL | 2006

A recent coincidence caught my eye while at the bookstore. A new book by Karim Rashid called *Design Your Self* was sitting on the shelf next to a new magazine from Martha Stewart called *Blueprint*, which bore a similarly cheerful entreaty on its cover: "Design your life!" These two publications join Ellen Lupton's recent *DIY: Design It Yourself* to form a sort of mini-explosion of literature aimed at democratizing the practice of design (never mind that, as Lupton has noted, Rashid's book is actually more about designing his self than yours).

With the popularity of home improvement shows and self-help books, our society is positively awash in do-it-yourself spirit. People don't just eat food anymore, they present it; they don't look at pictures, they take them; they don't buy T-shirts, they sell them. People are doing-it-themselves to no end. But to what end? The artist Joe Scanlan touches on the more troubling implications of the DIY explosion in his brilliantly deadpan piece DIY, which is essentially instructions for making a perfectly functional coffin out of an IKEA bookcase.

Scanlan's piece accepts the basic assumption of "Design your life" and *Design Your Self*: that design is something that anyone can (and should) partici-pate in. But what is behind all this doing-it-ourselves? Does that coffin have your career's name on it?

The design-your-life mind-set is part of a wider cultural and economic phenomenon that I call *prosumerism*—simultaneous production and consumption. The confluence of work and leisure is common to a lot of hobbies, from scrap-booking to hot-rodding. But what was once a niche market has exploded in the last decade. Prosumerism is distinctly different from purchasing the tools for a do-it-yourself project. The difference can be seen most clearly in online products like Flickr and Wikipedia. These products embody an emerging form of inverted consumerism where the consumer provides the parts and the labor. In *The Wealth of Networks*, Yale Law School professor Yochai Benkler calls this inversion "social production" and says it is the first potent manifestation of the much-hyped information economy. Call it what you will, this "non-market activity" is changing not just the way people share information but their definition of what a product is.

This evolving consumer mentality might be called "the templated mind." The templated mind searches for text fields, metatags, and rankings like the handles on a suitcase. Data entry and customization options are the way prosumers grip this new generation of products. The templated mind hungers for customization and the opportunity to add their input—in essence to do-it-themselves. The templated mind trusts the result of social production more than the crafted messages of designers and copywriters. And this mentality is changing the design of products. Consider Movable Type, the software behind the blog revolution in general and this site in particular. This prosumer product has allowed hundreds of thousands of people to publish themselves on the web. For millions of people, their unconscious image of a website has been shaped by the constrained formats allowable by Movable Type templates. They unconsciously orient themselves to link and comments—they recognize the handiwork of a fellow prosumer. Any designer working on a webpage has to address that unconscious image. And it does not just impact designers in terms of form and style. As the template mentality spreads, consumers approach all products with the expectation of work. They are looking for the blanks, scanning for fields, checking for customization options, choosing their phone wallpaper, rating movies on Netflix, and uploading pictures of album art to Amazon. The template mentality emphasizes work over style or even clarity.

This shift in emphasis has the potential to marginalize designers. Take book covers. The rich tradition of cover design has developed because publishers have believed that a cover could help sell more books. But now more and more people are buying books based on peer reviews, user

THE SURPRISING BY-PRODUCT OF THIS DEMOCRATIZATION OF DISTRIBUTION IS THAT THE PRODUCTION/CONSUMPTION CYCLE HAS SPLINTERED INTO MILLIONS OF TINY EXCHANGES.

DMITRI SIEGEL
Comment from
"Designing Our
Own Graves"
2006

recommendations, and rankings. Word of mouth has always been a powerful marketing force, but now those mouths have access to sophisticated networks on which their words can spread faster than ever before. Covers are seen at 72 dpi at best. The future of the medium depends on how it is integrated into the process of social production. The budget that once went to design fees is already being redirected to manipulating search criteria and influencing Google rankings. A good book cover can still help sell books, but it is up against a lot more competition for the marketing dollar.

Prosumerism is also changing the role of graphic design in the music industry. When the music industry made the shift to compact discs in the late 1980s, many designers complained that the smaller format would be the death of album art. Fifteen years later those predictions seem almost quaint. The MP3 format makes compact disc packaging seem like the broad side of a barn. The "it" bands of the last few years—Arctic Monkeys, Clap Your Hands Say Yeah, and Gnarls Barkley to name just a few—have all broken into the popular consciousness via file sharing. Arctic Monkeys and CYHSY generated huge buzz on MySpace before releasing records, and Gnarls Barkley's irresistible hit "Crazy" made it to the top of the UK pop charts before it was even released, based entirely on MP3 downloads. The cover art for the new album from the Yeah Yeah Yeahs was the result of a do-it-yourself flag project the band ran online. The public image of a musician or band is no longer defined by an artfully staged photo or eye-popping album art. A file name that fits nicely into the "listening to" field in the MySpace template might be more important. The MP3 format and the ubiquity of downloading has shrunk the album art canvas to a 200 x 200–pixel JPEG. Music videos, once the ultimate designer dream gig, have shrunk as well. Imagine trying to watch M&Co.'s "Nothing But Flowers" video for the Talking Heads on a video iPod. As playlists and favorites become the currency of the music industry, the album as an organizing principle may disappear entirely. Soon graphic designers may only be employed to create 6 x 6–pixel favicons.

In *Revolutionary Wealth*, veteran futurists Alvin and Heidi Toffler (*Future Shock*, *The Third Wave*) paint a very optimistic picture of prosumerism. They rightly make the connection between the do-it-yourself ethos and the staggering increases in wealth that have occurred around the world in the last century. They describe a future where people use their extraordinary accumulated wealth to achieve greater and greater autonomy from industrial and corporate production. Benkler also spends a great deal of time celebrating the increased freedom and autonomy that social production provides.

But is the unimpeded spread of this kind of autonomy really possible? Benkler raises serious concerns about efforts to control networks through private ownership and legislation. Wikipedia is not a kit that you buy; you do not own your Flickr account and you never will. When you update a MySpace account you are building up someone else's asset. The prosumer model extracts the value of your work in real time, so that you are actually consuming your own labor.

And what would be the role of the designer in a truly do-it-yourself economy? Looking at Flickr or YouTube or MySpace, it seems that when people do it themselves, they need a great deal less graphic design to get it done. The more that our economy runs on people doing it themselves, the more people will demand opportunities to do so, and the more graphic designers will have to adapt their methods. What services and expertise do designers have to offer in the prosumer market? Rashid and Lupton have provided one answer (the designer as expert do-it-yourselfer), but unless designers come up with more answers, they may end up designing-it-themselves...and little else.

JESSICA HELFAND SEIZED THE SLIPPERY REINS OF NEW MEDIA WHILE IT WAS STILL IN ITS INFANCY. She took on interactive design in the 1990s through website design, online identities, and her media column, "Screen," in *Eye* magazine. In 2003 she joined William Drenttel (her husband and business partner), Michael Bierut, and Rick Poynor to create the blog Design Observer, an intellectual nexus for online debate and discussion of graphic design. To Helfand, the web is the new frontier, and designers need the guts to take it on. In the essay below she demands, "Where is the avant-garde in new media?" She herself sets a bold example. From Winterhouse, their rural Connecticut studio, Helfand and Drenttel write, edit, publish, educate, and design. They embody evolving models of graphic authorship as they crisscross the worlds of print and new media. Their personal library of around eight thousand volumes informs their work both practically and theoretically. In 1994 Helfand became a critic at Yale School of Art. She says of the design profession, "Somehow, I think graphic design succeeds best when it resists definition."[1]

1 Jessica Helfand interview in Debbie Millman, *How to Think Like a Great Graphic Designer* (New York: Allsworth Press, 2007), 147.

DEMATERIALIZATION OF SCREEN SPACE

JESSICA HELFAND | 2001

From the fifteenth through the early twentieth centuries, our understanding of space and time was bound by an unflinching belief in the four cornerstones of physical reality, framed by what is routinely considered to be a kind of Newtonian paradigm: space, time, energy, and mass. Like Euclidean space, which defines directional thinking in vectors (top, bottom, left, and right), the Western concept of space was absolute: boundless and infinite, flat and inert, knowable and fixed.

Then in 1905, Albert Einstein revolutionized five hundred years of quantum physics by suggesting that energy and mass are interchangeable, and that space and time share a kind of uninterrupted continuum—proving, quite simply, that the only true constant is the speed of light.

Today, as we sit illuminated by the glare of a billion computer screens, we are living proof that he was right. The computer is our connection to the world. It is an information source, an entertainment device, a communications portal, a production tool. We design on it and for it, and are its most loyal subjects, its most agreeable audience. But we are also its prisoners: trapped in a medium in which visual expression must filter through a protocol of uncompromising programming scripts, "design" must submit

I THINK STYLE HAS A WAY OF SUPERSEDING CONTENT, THAT THE RISE AND PROLIFERATION OF INDIVIDUAL TECHNOLOGIES HAVE HAD A NEGATIVE EFFECT ON HUMAN CIVILITY; AND I THINK THAT DESIGNERS ARE GETTING COMPLACENT. BUT THAT'S JUST TODAY.

JESSICA HELFAND
Interview with
Debbie Millman
2007

to a series of commands and regulations as rigorous as those that once defined Swiss typography. Aesthetic innovation, if indeed it exists at all, occurs within ridiculously preordained parameters: a new plug-in, a modified code, the capacity to make pictures and words "flash" with a mouse in a nonsensical little dance. We are all little filmmakers, directing on a pathetically small screen—yet broadcasting to a potentially infinite audience. This in itself is conflicting (not to mention corrupting), but more importantly, what are we making? What are we inventing? What are we saying that has not been said before?

WHERE IS THE AVANT-GARDE IN NEW MEDIA?

What Einstein did was challenge a fundamentally logical supposition. And looking back, what was particularly striking was the aesthetic response that paralleled his thinking over the next quarter of a century: from cubist fragmentation, to surrealist displacement, to futurist provocation, to constructivist juxtaposition—each, in a sense, a radically new reconsideration of spatial paradigms in a material world. And while there was dissent, there was also consensus: streamlined shapes, a rejection of ornament, an appeal to minimalism, to functionalism, to simplicity. A response to the machine age—not just to the machine.

It is, of course, a particular conceit of postmodernism that a lack of consensus is precisely what separates the second half of the twentieth century from the first. But does this alone explain the creative disparity so evident in electronic space? More likely, it is not space that demands our attention now so much as our representation of space, and our ability to mold and manage ideas within boundaries that are fundamentally intangible: what we need is a reconsideration of spatial paradigms in an immaterial world.

To date, our efforts to define space on the Internet have required a basic fluency in the fundamental markup languages that are needed to bring design to life; SGML, HTML, XML, WAP protocols, and soon, with the imminent convergence of television and the web, TVML. Each deals in linear, logical, Cartesian alignments: ones and zeroes, x's and y's, pull-down menus and scrolling screens. Supporting software products remain essentially rooted in the finite world of printed matter: most are based on editing and publishing models and, not surprisingly, have a page-oriented display system, adding additional "media" as needed to extend or evoke information beyond the customary offerings of text and image. And though they purport to be more multidimensional in nature, architectural opportunities to place 3D models in "space" offer little more than sculptural simulations, providing basic toolsets for rotating geometric forms that mimic movement in a primitive, awkward, cartoony sort of way.

Nowhere do we see the kind of variety, or depth, or topographical distinctions we might expect, given the boundless horizons of Internet space. Nowhere do we see a new spatial paradigm, an alternative way of representing ideas—of experimenting, for example, with what philosopher Gaston Bachelard lyrically refers to as "the psychological elasticity of an image." Nowhere do we see, or feel, or discover a new sense of place, freed of the shackles of Cartesian logic—space that might ebb and flow, expand and contract, dimensional space, elliptical space, new and unusual space. Homepages, indeed! What could possibly be said to be homey about the web—or even about TV, for that matter? Do we find shelter, permanence, or comfort there? Does it smell good? Is it warm, familiar, personal? What domestic truths are mirrored in the space of the screen, projected back to us, and beamed elsewhere?

This is one of the more irritating myths about the electronic age, yet one that perpetually seems to reinstate itself with each new technological advance. Space on the screen is just that: on the screen. Not in it. Not of it. Design tools are mere control mechanisms perpetuating the illusion that Internet space is made up of pages, of words, of flat screens. Why is it that design thinking remains so brainwashed by this notion? The world of the Internet is its own peculiar galaxy, with its own constellations of information, its own orbits of content. And it is by no means flat.

DISPLACEMENT (OF THE OBSERVER)

The rectangle of the computer monitor frames everything we see on screen. Our peripheral vision is at all times influenced—if not altogether compromised—by the stultifying presence of the container, an unforgiving geometry if there ever was one. (Oddly, this same frame circumscribes the photographer looking through the camera lens—yet here, the frame itself fades from view the minute the shutter clicks. Not so when the mouse clicks, however.) More puzzling still, the lure of networked interaction on the web is predicated on precisely the opposite set of conditions: though circumscribed by a steadfast box, virtual space celebrates the intangible gesture, the dematerialized transaction, the inconquerable, timeless exchange.

What has not been recognized is the extent to which the viewer is a moving target. Are our conceptions of electronic space lodged in geometric exactitude in an effort to harness the dynamic of an unruly audience?

NATURE ABHORS A VACUUM, AND SO SHOULD DESIGNERS: HISTORY
IS AN IMPERATIVE PART OF HOW WE WORK, WHAT WE MAKE, AND HOW
WE CONTINUE TO GROW AS DESIGNERS AND AS HUMAN BEINGS.

JESSICA HELFAND
Interview with Cary
Murnion in *Baseline:
Journal of Parsons
School of Design*
1997

Efforts to break out of the box—and here some of the experimental studies conducted at places like the MIT Media Lab, among other schools and research facilities, merit attention—have addressed this conflict by creating what might broadly be characterized as "ambient" media: websites projected on walls, push-button and hand-held devices replaced by portable, mutable media that gesture and respond to sensory input—all are attempts both to reinterpret and reinforce monitor-free interaction between human beings and the machines that serve them.

But this trend in portability points to a broader, more significant cultural phenomenon: in an age in which perception itself is synonymous with transience, we remain more preoccupied with the space surrounding the *technology* than with the space inside the technology.

Though this is particularly true of the Internet, our understanding of television space is not dissimilar. Here, too, we chart the course, control the path, and click our way through a kind of visual no-man's land. What has not been examined is the degree to which our spatial perception skews, like a reflex, as if to automatically compensate for the fragmented nature of the journey.

DEMATERIALIZATION (OF WHAT IS BEING OBSERVED)

What is missing from Internet space is not only a defining set of physical boundaries but the temporal references that give implicit direction—meaning, even—to our actions. Not so in the 24-7 space of the Internet, where space and time do, in fact, share an uninterrupted continuum, and where the conventions of timekeeping—clocks, calendars, the occasional sunrise—are rendered virtually immaterial. (The television tactic of rationalizing time through programming will itself be rendered somewhat immaterial as well if the promises of webTV are fulfilled. The introduction of TiVo—"TV your way"—is the first significant step in this direction.) More interesting, perhaps, is the shape of things as they are happening: indeed, the qualitative difference between hyperspace and more passive screen environments (television and film, for example) lies in the celebration of the journey itself. In interactive environments, the promenade—and its implicit digressions—are as important as the destination.

This is as close to a definition of "vernacular" as we are likely to get in electronic space: if the viewer moves through the information, and the information itself is moving, it is this kinetic activity—this act of moving—that circumscribes our perception, dominates our senses, and becomes, in a very noticeable sense, the new prevailing aesthetic.

DEMARCATION (OF NEW BOUNDARIES)

It is easy to equate the notion of wide, open spaces with freedom and opportunity—qualities that we associate with the bold ambitions of early settlers, of westward expansion and manifest destiny and the inimitable American frontier. Such pioneering spirit has long retained its almost mythic status in modern culture, symbolizing freedom, individualism, and a kind of peculiarly American democracy.

Like the once-open West, Internet space is uncharted territory. Air is free and land is cheap. And, indeed, its presence in our lives points to a kind of utopian idealism prefigured a century ago, when we thrilled to the notion of pure, mechanized efficiency.

But today, the boundaries have shifted. New boundaries are enabled by new kinds of technologies, by the demands of new products and the imperatives of new economies. The Internet is all these: a kind of chameleon-like civilization that seems to perpetually remap its identity in response to the ever-changing demands of a mercurial market. In a world in which everything is customized, even our boundaries are on the move.

So it all fits together: portable media, transient journeys, movable boundaries. Unlike our nineteenth-century predecessors we have not shaped this new world with nuance and detail, with an urban-industrial east or a preservationist west. We have not responded with a hue and cry borne of the kind of revolutionary fervor typified by early-twentieth-century designers and artists. More likely, our response has been a reactive one: to technological imperatives, to pragmatic considerations, and to each other. To think beyond these practicalities is to respond to a broader and more compelling challenge: the idea that, as designers, we might begin to tackle the enormous opportunities to be had in staking claim to and shaping a new and unprecedented universe. There, if anywhere, lies the new avant-garde.

NYA HARA GREW UP IN TOKYO, WHERE HIS FATHER WAS BOTH A BUSINESSMAN AND A SHINTO PRIEST. Hara himself draws deeply from the Japanese traditions of "emptiness and potentiality" so integral to Shinto.[1] Out of such traditions Hara creates impeccable graphic design that replaces frenzied technology-driven experience with sensory-driven design. In his 2007 book, *Designing Design*, from which the essay below is taken, he provides an alternative to the voracious Western appetite for "newness." In his words, "Design is…the originality that repeatedly extracts astounding ideas from the crevices of the very commonness of everyday life."[2] He urges designers to stop straining to keep up with technology and instead begin to experience anew the world in which we actually live. "Human happiness," he explains, "lies in how fully we can savor our living environment."[3] A designer, author, curator, and educator, Hara leads an emerging powerhouse of Japanese designers. As creative director for the Japanese company MUJI, he oversees the design development of hundreds of products for home and office. There he has crafted a global strategy for marketing and advertising that expresses the company's "no-brand" philosophy. In addition, Hara is managing director of the prestigious Nippon Design Center.

1 See interview with Maggie Kinser Hohle, "Kenya Hara: Praise the Gap," *Graphis* (July–August 2002): 32–53.

2 Kenya Hara, *Designing Design*, trans. Maggie Kinser Hohle and Yukiko Naito (Baden: Lars Müller, 2007), 435.

3 Kenya Hara, interview with Maggie Kinser Hohle, "Kenya Hara: MUJI Creative Director," *Theme* 3 (Fall 2005), http://www.thememagazine.com (accessed February 1, 2008).

DESIGNING DESIGN

KENYA HARA | 2007

COMPUTER TECHNOLOGY AND DESIGN

Where does design stand today? The remarkable progress of information technology has thrown our society into great turmoil. The computer promises, we believe, to dramatically increase human ability, and the world has overreacted to potential environmental change in that computer-filled future. In spite of the fact that our rockets have only gone as far as the moon, the world busies itself with worries and preparations for intergalactic travel.

The cold war between East and West is over, and the world long ago began revolving on the unspoken standard of economic might. In a world in which economic power accounts for the majority of our values, people believe that the best plan for preserving that power is to respond quickly to forecasted changes to the environment. Convinced of a paradigm shift to rival the Industrial Revolution, people are so worried about missing the bus that they beat their brains out trying to get to a new place, but are only acting on precepts of precomputer education.

In a world in which the motive force is the desire to get the jump on the next person, to reap the wealth computer technology is expected to yield, people have no time to leisurely enjoy the actual benefits and treasures already available, and in leaning so far forward in anticipation of the possibilities, they've lost their balance and are in a highly unstable situation, barely managing to stay upright as they fall forward into their next step.

Apparently, people think they shouldn't criticize technological progress. It may be that deeply seated in the consciousness of our contemporaries is an obsession of a sort, to the effect that those who contradicted the Industrial Revolution or the machine civilization were thought of as lacking in foresight and were looked down upon. That's why people have such a hard time speaking out against flaws that are likely felt by everyone. This is probably because they're afraid that anyone who grumbles about technology will be thought an anachronism. Society has no mercy for those who can't keep up with the times.

However, at the risk of being misunderstood, I have to say that technology ought to evolve more slowly and steadily. It would be best if it took the time to mature, through trial and error. We are so excessively and frantically competitive that we have repeatedly planted unsteady systems in unsteady ground, which have evolved into a variety of trunk systems that are weak and liable to fail, but have been left to develop anyway. Having no way to stop, they barrel down the track, completely exhausted. People have wrapped themselves in this unhealthy technological environment and are accumulating more stress every day. Technology continues to advance and has multiplied beyond the amount knowable by a single individual; its entirety can be neither grasped nor seen, and it's so vast its edges fade from view. There is nothing aesthetically appealing about communication or the practice of making things when their ideology and education remain unable to cope with this situation, but just continue on their familiar trodden paths.

The computer is not a tool but a material. So says John Maeda, a professor at the Massachusetts Institute of Technology. The implication is that we shouldn't use computers in the manner of just swallowing whatever software comes along, but need to think deeply and carefully about what kind of intellectual world can be cultivated based on this new material that operates with numbers. I think his suggestion deserves our respect. For any material to become a superb material, we need to purify its distinguishing attributes as much as possible. As a material for modeling and carving, clay has endless plasticity, but that limitless plasticity is not unrelated to the material's development. If it were filled with nails or other shards of metal, we wouldn't be able to knead it to a usable consistency. These days it's as if we're kneading the clay until our hands bleed. I have trouble believing that anything generated in this kind of impossible situation is going to bring any satisfaction to our lives.

Design today has been given the role of presenting the latest innovations of technology and here, too, is strained. Design, which is accustomed to showing its strength in "making what's fresh today look old tomorrow" as well as bringing novel fruits to a table full of curious diners, is further exacerbating its contortions, in obedience to the new technology.

BEYOND MODERNISM

Digging a little deeper into the relationship between technology and communication, some designers have begun to rethink the possibilities of the quality of information; putting aside the rough information that swirls around like dust on the Internet and clings to our monitors, they have recognized the profundity of the quality of information perceptible only when the senses become mobilized. A symbolic example is the attention in recent years that the field of cognitive science (which studies virtual reality) has showered on the "haptic" senses—those besides sight and hearing. The very delicate human senses have begun to become very important in the forefront of technology. Human beings and the environment being equally tangible, the comfort as well as the satisfaction we sense is based on how we appreciate and cherish our communication with the world via our diverse sensory organs. In terms of this perspective, the paired fields of design and technology and of design and science are headed in the same direction. I specialize in communication but have come to think that the ideal of this discipline is not trying to catch the audience's eye with an arresting image, but having the image permeate the five senses. This is communication that is very elusive yet solid and therefore tremendously powerful, which succeeds before we even realize it's there.

LEV MANOVICH ADDRESSES NEW MEDIA THROUGH WORK THAT IS BOTH HIGHLY THEORETICAL AND IMMINENTLY PRACTICAL. This Moscow-born artist is also a commercial designer, animator, programmer, author, and educator. His texts, published primarily online, are developed side by side with art experiments that include conceptual software, streaming novels, and database-supported films. In the essay below, he shakes graphic design's aesthetic foundations, pointing to a fundamental transformation in our shared visual language. As Manovich explains, specific techniques, artistic languages, and vocabularies previously isolated within individual professions are being imported and exported across software applications and professions to create shared "metamedia." This new common language of hybridity and "remixability," through which most visual artists now work, is unlike anything seen before. Manovich is a professor at the University of California, San Diego, where he teaches both practical courses in digital art and theoretical courses in digital culture.

IMPORT/EXPORT, OR DESIGN
WORKFLOW AND CONTEMPORARY AESTHETICS

LEV MANOVICH | 2008

Although "import"/"export" commands appear in most modern media authoring and editing software running under GUI, at first sight they do not seem to be very important for understanding software culture. You are not authoring new media or modifying media objects or accessing information across the globe, as in web browsing. All these commands allow you to do is to move data around between different applications. In other words, they make data created in one application compatible with other applications. And that does not look so glamorous.

Think again. What is the largest part of the economy of the greater Los Angeles area? It is not entertainment—from movie production to museums and everything in between (around 15%). It turns out that the largest part is the import/export business (more than 60%). More generally, one commonly evoked characteristic of globalization is greater connectivity—places, systems, countries, organizations, etc. becoming connected in more and more ways. And connectivity can only happen if you have a certain level of compatibility: between business codes and procedures, between shipping technologies, between network protocols, and so on.

Let us take a closer look at import/export commands. As I will try to show below, these commands play a crucial role in software culture, and in particular in media design. Because my own experience is in visual media, my examples

LEV MANOVICH
"After Effects, or
Velvet Revolution
in Modern Culture.
Part 1"
2006

will come from this area, but the processes I describe apply now to all media designed with software.

Before they adopted software tools in the 1990s, filmmakers, graphic designers, and animators used completely different technologies. Therefore, as much as they were influenced by each other or shared the same aesthetic sensibilities, they inevitably created different-looking images. Filmmakers used camera and film technology designed to capture three-dimensional physical reality. Graphic designers were working with offset printing and lithography. Animators were working with their own technologies: transparent cells and an animation stand with a stationary film camera capable of making exposures one frame at a time as the animator changed cells and/or moved backgrounds.

As a result, twentieth-century cinema, graphic design, and animation (I am talking here about standard animation techniques used by commercial studios) developed distinct artistic languages and vocabularies in terms of both form and content. For example, graphic designers worked with a two-dimensional space, film directors arranged compositions in three-dimensional space, and cell animators worked with a "two-and-a-half" dimensional space. This holds for the overwhelming majority of works produced in each field, although of course exceptions do exist. For instance, Oskar Fischinger made one abstract film that involved moving three-dimensional shapes—but as far as I know, this is the only time in the whole history of abstract animation where we see an abstract three-dimensional space.

The differences in technology influenced what kind of content would appear in different media. Cinema showed "photorealistic" images of nature, built environments and human forms articulated by special lighting. Graphic designs feature typography, abstract graphic elements, monochrome backgrounds, and cutout photographs. And cartoons show hand-drawn flat characters and objects animated over hand-drawn but more detailed backgrounds. The exceptions are rare. For instance, while architectural spaces frequently appear in films because they could explore their three dimensionality in staging scenes, they practically never appear in animated films in any detail—until animation studios start using 3D computer animation.

Why was it so difficult to cross boundaries? For instance, in theory one could imagine making an animated film in the following way: printing a series of slightly different graphic designs and then filming them as though they were a sequence of animated cells. Or a film where a designer simply made a series of hand drawings that used the exact vocabulary of graphic design and then filmed them one by one. And yet, to the best of my knowledge, such a film was never made. What we find instead are many abstract animated films that

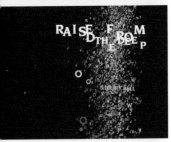

PETER ANDERSON *Raised from the Deep*, title sequence for Channel Four documentary, 2001.

have certain connections to various styles of abstract painting. For example, Oskar Fischinger's films and paintings share certain forms. We can find abstract films and animated commercials and movie titles that have certain connections to graphic design of the times. For instance, some moving image sequences made by motion graphics pioneer Pablo Ferro around 1960s display psychedelic aesthetics that can be also found in posters, record covers, and other works of graphic design in the same period.

And yet, it is never exactly the same language. One reason is that projected film could not adequately show the subtle differences between typeface sizes, line widths, and grayscale tones crucial for modern graphic design. Therefore, when the artists were working on abstract art films or commercials that used design aesthetics (and most key abstract animators produced both), they could not simply expand the language of printed page into time dimension. They had to invent essentially a parallel visual language that used bold contrasts, more easily readable forms, and thick lines—which because of their thickness were in fact no longer lines but shapes.

Although the limitations in resolution and contrast of film and television image in contrast to the printed page played a role in keeping the distance between the languages used by abstract filmmakers and graphic designers for most of the twentieth century, ultimately I do not think they were the decisive factor. Today the resolution, contrast, and color reproduction between print, computer screens, and television screens are also substantially different—and yet we often see exactly the same visual strategies deployed across these different display media. If you want to be convinced, leaf through any book or magazine on contemporary 2D design (i.e., graphic design for print, broadcast, and the web). When you look at a spread featuring the works of a particular designer or a design studio, in most cases it's impossible to identify the origins of the images unless you read the captions. Only then do you find that this image is a poster, that one is a still from a music video, and this one is magazine editorial.

I am going to use Taschen's *Graphic Design for the 21st Century: 100 of the World's Best Graphic Designers* (2003) for examples. Peter Anderson's images [left] showing a heading against a cloud of hundreds of little letters in various orientations turn out to be the frames from the title sequence for a Channel Four documentary. His other image [page 131], which similarly plays on the contrast between jumping letters in a larger font against irregularly cut planes made from densely packed letters in much smaller fonts, turns to be a spread from IT magazine. Since the first design was made for broadcast while the second was made for print, we would expect that the first design would employ bolder forms—however, both designs use the same scale between big and small fonts and feature texture fields composed from text that no longer need to be read. […]

These designs rely on software's ability (or on the designer being influenced by software use and following the same logic while doing the design manually) to treat text as any graphical primitive and to easily create compositions made from hundreds of similar or identical elements positioned according to some pattern. And since an algorithm can easily modify each element in the pattern, changing its position, size, color, etc., instead of the completely regular grids of modernism we see more complex structures that are made from many variations of the same element.

[…]

Everybody who is practically involved in design and art today knows that contemporary designers use the same set of software tools to design everything. However, the crucial factor is not the tools themselves but the workflow process, enabled by "import" and "export" operations.

When a particular media project is being put together, the software used at the final stage depends on the type of output media and the nature of the project—for instance, After Effects for motion graphics projects and video compositing, Illustrator or Freehand for print illustrations, InDesign for graphic design, Flash for interactive interfaces and web animations, 3ds Max or Maya for 3D computer models and animations. But these programs are rarely used alone to create a media design from start to finish. Typically, a designer may create elements in one program, import them into another program, add elements created in yet another program, and so on. This happens regardless of whether the final product is an illustration for print, a website, or a motion graphics sequence; whether it is a still or a moving image, interactive or noninteractive, etc. Given this production workflow, we may expect that the same visual techniques and strategies will appear in all media designed with computers.

For instance, a designer can use Illustrator or Freehand to create a 2D curve (technically, a spline). This curve becomes a building block that can be used in any project. It can form a part of an illustration or a book design. It can be imported into an animation program where it can be set to motion, or imported into a 3D program where it can be extruded in 3D space to define a solid form.

Each of the types of programs used by media designers—3D graphics, vector drawing, image editing, animation, compositing—excel at particular design operations, i.e., particular ways of creating a design element or modifying an already existing element. These operations can be compared to the different blocks of a Lego set. While you can make an infinite number of projects out of these blocks, most of the blocks will be utilized in every project, although they will have different functions and appear in different combinations. For example, a rectangular red block may become a part of a tabletop, part of the head of a robot, etc.

Design workflow that uses multiple software programs works in a similar way, except in this case the building blocks are not just different kinds of visual elements one can create—vector patterns, 3D objects, particle systems, etc.—but also various ways of modifying these elements: blur, skew, vectorize, change transparency level, spherisize, extrude, etc. This difference is very important. If media creation and editing software did not include these and many other modification operations, we would have seen an altogether different visual language at work today. We would have seen "digital multimedia," i.e., designs that simply combine elements from different media. Instead, we see what I call "metamedia"—the remixing of working methods and techniques of different media within a single project.

Here are a few typical examples of this media "remixability" that can be seen in the majority of design projects done today around the world. Motion blur is applied to 3D computer graphics; computer-generated fields of particles are blended with live-action footage to give it an enhanced look, flat drawings are placed into a virtual space where a virtual camera moves around them, flat typography is animated as though it is made from a liquid-like material (the liquid simulation coming from computer animation software). Today a typical short film or a sequence may combine many of such pairings within the same frame. The result is a hybrid, intricate, complex, and rich media language—or, rather, numerous languages that share the basic logic of remixability.

As we can see, the production workflow specific to the software age has two major consequences: the hybridity of media language we see today across the contemporary design universe, and the use of the similar techniques and strategies regardless of the output media and type of project. Like an object built from Lego blocks, a typical design today combines techniques coming

PETER ANDERSON *Moving Surnames, Northern Ireland series 2*, Treble page spread, *IT Magazine.*

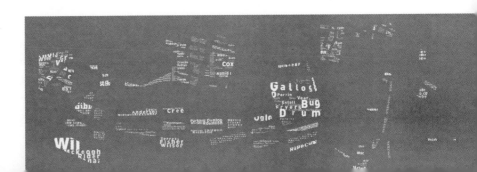

LEV MANOVICH
"After Effects, or
Velvet Revolution
in Modern Culture.
Part 1"
2006

from multiple media. More precisely, it combines the results of the operations specific to different software programs that were originally created to imitate work with different physical media. (Illustrator was created to make illustrations, Photoshop to edit digitized photographs, After Effects to create 2D animation, etc.) While these techniques continue to be used in relation to their original media, most of them are now also used as part of the workflow on any design job.

The essential condition that enables this new design logic and the resulting aesthetics is compatibility between files generated by different programs. In other words, "import" and "export" commands of graphics, animation, video editing, compositing, and modeling software are historically more important than the individual operations these programs offer. The ability to combine raster and vector layers within the same image, to place 3D elements into a 2D composition and vice versa, and so on is what enables the production workflow with its reuse of the same techniques, effects, and iconography across different media.

The consequences of this compatibility between software and file formats, which was gradually achieved during the 1990s, are hard to overestimate. Besides the hybridity of modern visual aesthetics and reappearance of exactly the same design techniques across all output media, there are also other effects. For instance, the whole field of motion graphics as it exists today came into existence to a large extent because of the integration between vector-drawing software, specifically Illustrator, and animation/compositing software such as After Effects. A designer typically defines various composition elements in Illustrator and then imports them into After Effects, where they are animated. This compatibility did not exist when the initial versions of different media authoring and editing software initially became available in the 1980s. It was gradually added in particular software releases. But when it was achieved around the middle of the 1990s, within a few years the whole language of contemporary graphic design was fully imported into the moving-image area—both literally and metaphorically.

In summary, the compatibility between graphic design, illustration, animation, and visual effects software plays the key role in shaping visual and spatial forms of the software age. On the one hand, never before have we witnessed such a variety of forms as today. On the other hand, exactly the same techniques, compositions, and iconography can now appear in any media. And at the same time, any single design may combine multiple operations that previously only existed within distinct physical or computer media.

And you thought that "import"/"export" commands did not matter that much?

ELLEN LUPTON GAVE GRAPHIC DESIGN A NEW VOCABULARY. THROUGH HER SEMINAL BOOKS AND EXHIBITIONS, SHE TOOK KEY THEORETICAL IDEAS ENCOMPASSING ART, LITERATURE, AND CULTURE AND APPLIED THEM TO OUR PROFESSION. When people want to understand design, they turn to Lupton. Beginning in 1992, she served as contemporary design curator for the Cooper-Hewitt, National Design Museum. In 2003 she launched a graphic design MFA program in Baltimore at the Maryland Institute College of Art. Through her work at these institutions and through her prolific writing, she has opened up the discourse of design to the general public. As the tools of publishing become increasingly available, Lupton explains, design thinking becomes increasingly essential. Through a broader understanding of design, citizens can become communicators; consumers can become producers. She believes, as she asserts in the essay below, that graphic design "is a mode of thinking and doing that belongs to everyone on earth." This essay was written with Lupton's twin sister Julia, a renowned Shakespeare scholar who has become a DIY designer on the side. The Lupton twins have embarked on a series of books and projects focused on bringing design skills and design thinking to new audiences; "Univers Strikes Back" was their first coauthored published piece.

UNIVERS STRIKES BACK

ELLEN AND JULIA LUPTON | 2007

In Print magazine in 2002, Katherine McCoy challenged designers to support local cultures by practicing audience-centered design. McCoy was voicing the postmodern disillusion with universal design. "As a Modernist Swiss-school graphic designer in the late sixties," McCoy wrote, "I knew we were going to remake the world in Helvetica." Modernism sought a common language built on systems and modularity; in contrast, the postmodernists valorized the special idioms and dialects of cultures and subcultures.

Today, culture seems as much a problem as a solution. Differences in ideology, religion, and national identity are tearing apart communities, countries, and the world itself. Tribal hatreds and civil warfare as well as corporate greed and imperial arrogance are doing the damage. No longer satisfied by the cult of cultures, philosophers, theologians, journalists, and artists around the world are recovering the universal ideas embedded in their particular religious, national, or communal orientations, whether it's love of neighbor, the equality of citizens, human rights, or responsibility for a shared planet.

Kwame Anthony Appiah, the Princeton philosopher and ethicist born and raised in Ghana, has questioned the values of multiculturalism in the name of a new "cosmopolitanism," literally, "world citizenship." Kumasi, the thriving, multilingual capital of Ghana's Asante region, is populated by people of Asante,

Hausa, South Asian, Middle Eastern, and British descent. In a small village just twenty miles away, the population is more ethnically homogeneous, but the culture is nonetheless connected to the world. "The villagers," Appiah writes, "will have radios; you will probably be able to get a discussion going about the World Cup in soccer, Muhammad Ali, Mike Tyson, and hip hop." They'll be drinking Guinness and Coca-Cola as well as Star lager, Ghana's own beer. But, he notes, you'll hear the local language, not English, playing on the radio, and their favorite soccer teams will be Ghanaian. These villages may be connected globally, but their homogeneity "is still the local kind"—the same level and style of homogeneity, he writes provocatively, that you would find in a New Jersey suburb.[1]

1 Kwame Anthony Appiah, *Cosmopolitanism: Ethics in a World of Strangers* (New York: W. W. Norton, 2006), 102.

Appiah eloquently opposes the attempt to create artificial museums out of local cultures. The world, he argues, is made up of individuals, not of cultures. Individuals belong to a shared humanity and a global civilization as well as to a local community. A cosmopolitan place such as New York or Paris or Kumasi draws its energy from a mix of persons, inextricably connected with a larger world, who have the right to participate in a world discourse.

Postmodernists exposed the ideal of universal communication as naively utopian at best and oppressively colonial at worst. After World War II, ideas pioneered by the modernist avant-garde came to serve globalization, whose international branding campaigns allow international brands, from Coca-Cola and McDonald's to IKEA and Starbucks, to compete with indigenous goods and services. Witness, in New York City, the gradual disappearance of the classic Greek diner coffee cup, designed by Leslie Buck in 1963 for a Connecticut paper goods manufacturer; once a ubiquitous throwaway, the rise of Starbucks has rendered it a nostalgic museum-shop souvenir.

But can global design sometimes affirm cultural identity while enhancing millions of lives? Consider IKEA, a company that has integrated furniture design, manufacturing, and branding with the social trends of nomadic living, customization, and disposability. Objects such as the humble Klippan couch, designed by Lars Engman in 1980, make good on the democratic ideals of the early modernist designers. Whereas few Bauhaus products ever reached mass markets, the Klippan, selling for under $200, has found a place in over a million homes in dozens of regions around the world.

One could fault IKEA for spreading the monotony of globalization. Although IKEA is a global company, it maintains a distinct regional identity (think meatballs, lingonberries, and cured salmon). Founded in 1943, IKEA built its product line around a Scandinavian variant of modernism—comfortable, casual, and adaptable to individual tastes. IKEA soon established stores in other Scandinavian countries and then across Western Europe and beyond.

AGAINST THE OPACITY AND SINGULARITY OF UNIQUE VISUAL EXPRESSION...
IDEAS OF COMMONALITY, TRANSPARENCY, AND OPENNESS ARE BEING
REBORN AS INFORMATION SEEKS TO SHED ITS PHYSICAL BODY.

ELLEN LUPTON
Thinking with Type
2004

When IKEA built its first United States store in 1985, the company already had outlets in Hong Kong, Australia, Saudi Arabia, and Dubai. Wherever IKEA opens its doors, people line up outside. In contrast with Coca-Cola and McDonald's, companies that tune their marketing and their recipes to local tastes, IKEA's merchandise and store design are more or less uniform across the world. At the same time, their products reflect and acknowledge global influences. A current store display tucks a tiny Japanese tea room at the end of a galley kitchen, marrying Nordic and Asian modes of minimalism.

Take the case of clothing sizes. In 1958, the U.S. government standardized sizes so that consumers could shop more reliably. In 1983, in the face of the changing shape of American bodies, these standards were abandoned and companies set their own. When you choose a brand, you're choosing a whole bundle of identifiers—not just gender, but age, class, and lifestyle. Hanes are oversized for the underclass, while American Apparel is slimmed down for the youth market. Tim Kaeding, creative director for 7 for All Mankind, a California jeans company, confessed in a recent interview, "In the jeans world especially, size is not a precise science. It's almost an irrelevant, made-up number system." Whose fault is that, anyway? Consumers practice the art of denial in response to a diet of fast food carbonated by images of the rich and thin. Marketers are there to make us feel better and buy more. A return to universal sizing would lead to greater transparency for consumers and producers everywhere.

How does this argument bear on graphic design? Consider the template, which offers generic solutions to common problems in a lame bid to automate design. Designer Dmitri Siegel has criticized what he calls the "templated mind," which searches for blanks to fill out, wallpapers to customize, and products to rank and rate. The dismal templates of PowerPoint serve more to control production than to empower its users with tools for agile thinking, yielding wordy, gimmick-ridden documents.

Yet PowerPoint has become an indispensable tool because it crosses platforms, giving everyone from schoolchildren to mid-level executives access to multimedia authoring. The challenge for designers—a group that increasingly includes thoughtful users as well as professional typographers—is to disable the stylistic limitations of templates without forgoing the expanded access to the tools of communication. For what makes design "universal" today is not the clean lines of Helvetica, but rather the spread of software such as Photoshop, Flash, and After Effects to vast new user groups, not just around the world but down the hall and across the street.

Transparency, layering, and hybridity have been features of artistic practice, including typography and design, since at least the rise of commercial printing.

ELLEN LUPTON
Interview by Nicole
Bearman and Gabrielle
Eade for Design Hub
2007

What makes these principles new again in today's context is their ubiquitous accessibility through commonly available software. They have become, in a different way from Helvetica, universal. The new universality pursues not a fixed, closed totality but an open infinity. It emanates from particular situations, from individual users solving specific problems. Their quirks and their quandaries force design to change and expand.

Consider the attempt to define "universal design." Does "universal design" refer to a single language or a global, panlinguistic typeface? Does it promote common access to education, tools, and software? Does it enumerate shared standards and protocols that allow information to be easily exchanged? Does it demand designing for users with diverse physical and cognitive abilities? Does it delineate a basic form language capable of describing an infinite array of visual relationships? "Universal design" encompasses all of these reference points, many of which were not concerns during modern design theory's first wave.

Multiculturalism celebrates the ethnic, racial, or gender identities of designers and their audiences. But designers are also drawn together by design itself as a common language. Each reader of this magazine produces work informed by his or her cultural background. But we are also engaged in a common exploration of the language of design, itself shaped by a variety of discourses, from typography to music to religion. We are developing our particular voices as people—as men and women, as members of a generation, as participants in local communities and institutions, but also as practitioners of a global design discourse. Moreover, more and more, whether we like it or not, we must approach our audiences not only as consumers of our designs, but as contributors to the designed world. The baseline that draws us all together is design.

Universal design as it is emerging now, after postmodernism, is not a generic, neutral mode of communication. Rather, it is a visual language enmeshed in a technologically evolving communications environment stretched and tested by an unprecedented range of people. Individuals can engage this language on their own terms, infusing it with their own energy and sensibilities in order to create communications that are appropriate to particular publics and purposes. Just as the Asante people of Ghana enjoy both Coca-Cola and Star lager, people around the world have access to pencils, pens, and paint as well as Photoshop, HTML, and Processing. People around the world sit on IKEA's Klippan couch. They talk on cell phones (in many languages) and surf the Internet (using common protocols). Design is a visual language whose endless permutations result from the particularities of individuals, institutions, and locales that are increasingly connected to one another by acts of communication and exchange.

ELLEN LUPTON Spread from *Design Writing Research: Writing on Graphic Design*, 1996. Written and designed by Lupton and J. Abbott Miller, this influential book presents an early example of the contemporary move toward graphic designers as authors.

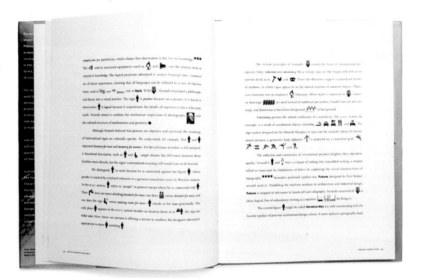

ELLEN LUPTON Spread from *Graphic Design: The New Basics*, 2008, written and designed by Ellen Lupton and Jennifer Cole Phillips. Through this book Lupton explores emerging universals within the practice of graphic design, including newly relevant concepts like transparency and layering.

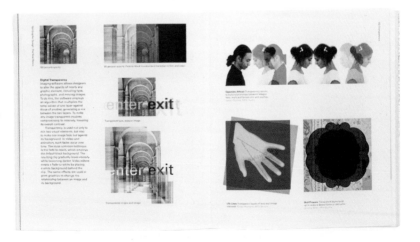

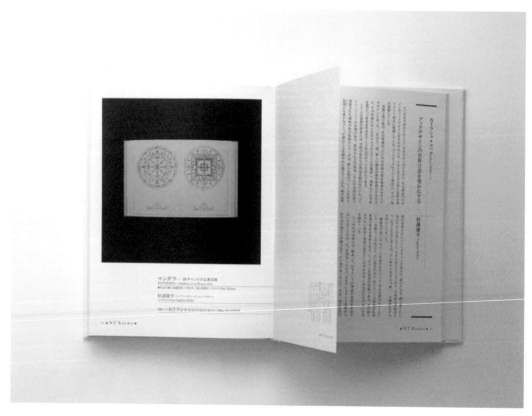

KENYA HARA *Paper and Design,* 2000. Book project for an exhibition to commemorate the centennial of the Takeo Paper Company. This project exemplifies Hara's reframing of books as "information sculpture." As he notes in *Designing Design,* "If electronic media is reckoned a practical tool for information conveyance, books are information sculpture; from now on, books will probably be judged according to how well they awaken that materiality, because the decision to create a book will be based on a definite choice of paper as the medium."[1]

1 Kenya Hara, *Designing Design,* trans. Maggie Kinser Hohle and Yukiko Naito (Baden: Lars Müller, 2007), 201.

KENYA HARA MUJI advertisements, 2003 (above) and 2004 (below). As creative director and advisory board member of MUJI, Hara does not advocate a philosophy of business and design meant to stir up individual desire. Instead, he embraces what he terms, "'global rational value,' a philosophy that advocates the use of resources and objects according to an exceedingly rational perspective."[1] MUJI advertising images suggest "moderation" and "detached reason," speaking not to the egotistical mind but the rational one.

1 Kenya Hara, *Designing Design*, trans. Maggie Kinser Hohle and Yukiko Naito (Baden: Lars Müller, 2007), 240.

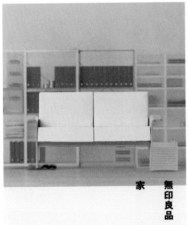

JAN VAN TOORN Spreads
from the visual essay "Panorama of Habits—Ten Everyday
Landscapes" in van Toorn's book,
Design's Delight, 2006. Each
spread is meant to be closely read
and interpreted by the reader.
Through such work van Toorn
suggests that designs are never
neutral. The designer should
expose the manipulation of the
message inherent in the work
and encourage readers to do
the same.

DMITRI SIEGEL Design for Nicholas Herman et al., *Russian Art in Translation*, 2007. This book is a catalog of emerging and established artists whose practice engages Russian identity and its complex legacy as a (failed) radical utopian state. Siegel produced this book through his publishing venture Ante Projects, which he founded with Herman in 2002 while they were students at the Yale University School of Art.

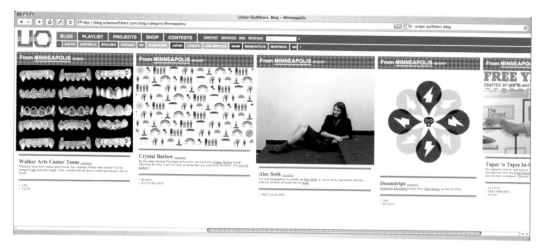

DMITRI SIEGEL Urban Outfitters Blog, 2008. The UO blog is the first horizontal scrolling blog in the history of the Internet. It compiles brand inspiration from around the world that can be easily filtered by city or keyword. Siegel designed the site to emphasize the uniqueness of authentic local "scenes," attempting to subvert the homogenizing tendency of many digital social networking sites. Blog formats like this illustrate what Siegel terms "postsumerism—the simultaneous production and consumption of content."

Logotype

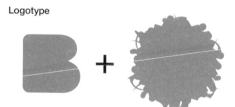

MICHAEL ROCK Identity for the Brooklyn Museum, 2004. Rock's Brooklyn identity, designed by his firm 2x4, is an early example of flexible logo systems that have since become popular. Such variable systems take full advantage of the multiple digital media now at play. Although some core visual remains consistent in such systems, the identity itself includes variable elements. The sharp contrast between the static controlled logos of twentieth-century designers like Paul Rand and new dynamic identities reflects the changing aesthetic emphasized by media theorist Lev Manovich.

Logotype Variations

Print Collateral

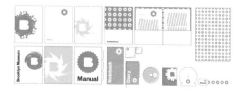

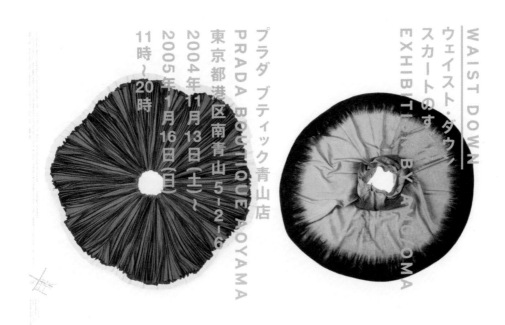

プラダ　ブティック青山店
PRADA BOUTIQUE AOYAMA
東京都港区南青山 5−2−6
2004年1月13日（土）〜
2005年1月16日（日）
11時〜20時

ウェイスト・ダウン／
スカートのす
EXHIBITION BY AMO OMA
WAIST DOWN

MICHAEL ROCK Poster from
Waist Down, a traveling exhibit
originally sited in the Prada Tokyo
Epicenter, 2004. Rock's firm, 2x4,
worked with exhibition designers
at OMA-AMO to develop the exhibit
and all collateral materials. Simultaneously working in Rotterdam,
Milan, New York, and Tokyo, 2x4
took full advantage of the current
global working climate. Such work
demonstrates the kind of collaboration for which Rock is known.

top: **JESSICA HELFAND, WILLIAM DRENTTEL, AND GEOFF HALBER** Spread from *Below the Fold,* Danger Issue, Fall 2005, published by the Winterhouse Institute. This self-initiated journal exemplifies the shift toward design authorship taking place within the graphic design industry, as well as within larger society. Each issue critically investigates a single topic through word and image.

right: **JESSICA HELFAND, WILLIAM DRENTTEL, AND BETSY VARDELL** The *New Yorker* website (redesign), 2007.

GLOSSARY

AVANT-GARDE Driven by utopian visions, avant-garde artists of the early twentieth century, particularly those discussed in the context of graphic design, sought new visual forms capable of objective, universal communication. These artists attempted to radically alter their own societies by merging art with everyday life, shifting the arts away from the individual, subjective, and, in their minds, corrupt visions of the past. Often the avant-garde used mass communication—books, magazines, exhibitions—to spread their ideals internationally.

BAUHAUS Under the leadership of Walter Gropius, this influential school opened in Weimar in 1919. Initially its express purpose was to merge art and craft, thereby elevating German industrial design. Although the experimental work there varied greatly, graphic designers usually focused on efforts by prominent Bauhaus members, including László Moholy-Nagy and Herbert Bayer, to uncover a universally comprehensible visual language. This quest greatly influenced New Typography. Also of note is the Bauhaus *Vorkurs*, or basic course, which became a curriculum model for art and design schools internationally, particularly in the United States. More generally, the Bauhaus has become synonymous with high modern design.

CONSTRUCTIVISM In 1921 a group of twenty-one Russian artists, inspired by Kazimir Malevich's *Black Square*, founded the Working Group of Constructivists. These artists put aside their easels, declaring that artists should produce only utilitarian art. The artist became the worker, the constructor. Founding members included Aleksandr Rodchenko, his partner Varvara Stepanova, Vladimir Tatlin, Aleksei Gan, and El Lissitzky. The movement's popularity faded in the USSR in the early 1930s after spreading across much of Europe.

CRAFT As digital technology increasingly dominates the creation and production of graphic design, a growing number of designers are looking instead to the physical act of making. They are incorporating a sense of the handmade into new technology or putting such technology aside altogether to explore older production methods like letterpress printing. In "The Macramé of Resistance," Lorraine Wild positions craft as central to a "designer's voice." For Wild, craft suggests a crucial knowledge acquired through making. She argues that this kind of knowledge, in addition to more verbal, conceptual approaches, must "form the foundation of a designer's education and work." Craft is often associated with the resurgence of ornament in the design community, as well as the broader DIY movement.

CRYSTAL GOBLET This well-known metaphor of typography is taken from Beatrice Warde's famous 1930 lecture, later published as an essay. According to Warde, typography should be beautifully transparent, communicating the message as clearly as possible while not calling attention to its own form.

CULTURE JAMMERS These activists use techniques of disruption to rebel against Corporate America's dominance of the media. They attack mainstream advertising through various techniques, including billboard liberation, media hoaxing, audio agitprop, subvertisements, and anti-ads. *Adbusters* magazine, founded by Kalle Lasn in 1989, has become a catalyst for culture jamming activities. See www.adbusters.org. A 1993 book entitled *Culture Jamming*, written by cultural critic Mark Dery, is the central text of the movement.

DEATH OF THE AUTHOR In 1967 French theorist Roland Barthes deconstructed the literary author's position as the originator of meaning through his concept of the death of the author. According to Barthes, instead of turning to the author to discern the meaning of a text, we should focus on the "open web of referents" in which the text functions. The author as the key producer of meaning was and is, in effect, dead. In the words of Barthes, "The birth of the reader must be at the cost of the death of the Author."

DECONSTRUCTION Jacques Derrida introduced the concept of deconstruction in his book *Of Grammatology* in France in 1967. In simplest terms deconstruction is a mode of questioning that breaks down the hierarchical oppositions of language, revealing its inherent instability. Within the design community this term is most widely applied to a complex, layered design style popular in the 1980s and 1990s that literally translated poststructuralist theories, including Derrida's key concept of deconstruction, into visual layouts. Involved work took place most notably at Cranbrook Academy of Art, where designers actively engaged the intricacies of poststructuralist thought within a broad body of work.

DIY (DO-IT-YOURSELF) MOVEMENT Supporters of this movement actively resist dependence on mass-produced goods and the multinational corporations that generally produce and distribute such goods. Instead participants encourage individuals to produce goods themselves, thereby protesting corporate exploitative labor and environmental practices while empowering individuals to become producers rather than just consumers.

FREE CULTURE MOVEMENT This social movement advocates a participatory rather than proprietary structure to society. To achieve this kind of open culture, participants put the power of communication, creation, and distribution into the hands of individuals by resisting and critiquing concepts of copyright and intellectual property. A crucial text for the movement is *Free Culture*, a book by Stanford University law professor Lawrence Lessig. The roots of the movement lie in the free software movement. See http://freeculture.org.

FUNCTIONALISM In the early 1900s, avant-garde artists stripped their work of anything useless and/or ornamental in favor of utilitarian, highly functional design. This approach evolved into the core modern tenet of "form follows function," still much quoted as the key component of effective design. Postmodernists rebelled against these standards at the end of the twentieth century. Functionalism resurged in popularity at the onset of the twenty-first century as the vast amount of information archived and communicated through digital technology foregrounded issues of interface and usability.

FUTURISM Led by poet F. T. Marinetti, futurists shook off nineteenth century conventions, using the arts instead to express their unique vision of the twentieth century, a vision dominated by speed, aggression, and war. Marinetti's radical typographic experimentation freed other avant-garde artists, including prominent members of the Bauhaus, to explore dynamic new typographic forms that engaged the machine aesthetic of the industrialized world.

GRAPHIC AUTHORSHIP This term was first used by Cranbrook Academy of Art director Katherine McCoy in 1990. During that period, the concept was used to explore a postmodern shift toward personal, expressive work. During the 2000s, however, the term took on new meaning as designers began to author texts of design history and theory, as well as initiate other entrepreneurial endeavors. Within this authorship model of graphic design the presence of a client is no longer key to the design process.

GRID Grids divide and order content. They are most notoriously associated with International Style or Swiss-style design. For practitioners of this influential design approach, complex, modular grids play a crucial role in establishing a tightly controlled design methodology. Although the popularity of grids peaked with Swiss style in the 1950s and 1960s, they have recently incited new interest, since the broad expanse of the web demands complex universal ordering mechanisms.

INTERNATIONAL STYLE This design ideology stems from a modernist, rational, systematic approach. Designers often use a limited typographic and color palette, carefully constructed modular grids, and objective imagery. Such designers put aside personal vision and become, instead, translators who clearly, objectively communicate the client message. This "valueless" approach helped professionalize the design field in the 1950s and 1960s, moving it away from the arts and into the semiscientific realm. Such systems were particularly useful for large-scale corporate identities that began to appear during that time.

LEGIBILITY WARS During the 1980s and 1990s a conflict broke out between modern and postmodern designers. Modernists advocated legibility as a key component of graphic design; postmodernists questioned this, sacrificing legibility when necessary to achieve visual impact. Steven Heller's essay "The Cult of the Ugly" was a touchstone for this debate.

METAMEDIA According to Lev Manovich all forms of new media are merging into a giant all-encompassing metamedia in which working methods and techniques of different media are remixed within a single project. This evolving metamedia is radically transforming contemporary aesthetics.

MODERNISM The Modern movement falls roughly between the 1860s and the 1970s. It is typically defined as artists' attempts to cope with a newly industrialized society. Modernism is progressive and often utopian, empowering humans to improve or remake their environments. Within modernism falls various other movements crucial to the development of graphic design. These include futurism, constructivism, and New Typography. The design community continues to debate the value of modernism, as basic modernist tenets still define conventional standards for effective design.

NEW MEDIA This term typically refers to the distribution of information by digital means. However, as Lev Manovich notes in *The Language of New Media,* the term can be more accurately broadened to include the transformation of all media, old and new, through using digital technology.

NEW TYPOGRAPHY Avant-garde approaches to typography—sans serif type, asymmetrical balance, conscious utilization of the optical nature of type, and so forth—were developed by artists all over Europe, but primarily at the Bauhaus. These approaches are often referred to as New Typography. László Moholy-Nagy used this term in his essay of the same name written in 1923. Jan Tschichold codified these ideas in his seminal work *The New Typography* in 1928.

NEW WAVE Often used interchangeably with postmodernism or late modernism. Designers typically associate New Wave design with Wolfgang Weingart, a leader of the second wave of Swiss typographic style. Through this New Wave Weingart rebelled against Swiss design luminaries of the 1950s and 1960s, pushing intuition and personal expression to the forefront of his work. Notable students are April Greiman and Dan Friedman.

POSTMODERNISM Postmodernists recognize that meaning is inherently unstable; there is no essence or center that one should strive to reach. The broad term *postmodernism* is closely associated with the critical field of poststructuralism. Within the design community it can be used to refer to a layered, complex style or a poststructuralist critical approach to design. The postmodern movement begins roughly in the 1960s. There is no definite end point, although most suggest we have already moved into a post-postmodern world. Critics describe postmodernism as either a reaction against or the ultimate continuation of modernism. Either way, postmodernism moves away from the quest for absolutes and universally applicable values that characterize modernism.

SOCIAL RESPONSIBILITY MOVEMENT Participants in this movement urge the graphic design community to confront the negative societal and environmental consequences of our rampant consumer culture. The "First Things First Manifesto 2000," initially signed by thirty-three influential designers, brought issues to the forefront of design discourse. The manifesto was published in numerous magazines and journals internationally and is still a controversial topic. Note that it was an updated version of the "First Things First" manifesto published by Ken Garland in 1964.

TYPOPHOTO László Moholy-Nagy uses this term in his book *Malerei, Photographie, Film (Painting, Photography, Film)* published in 1925. Typophoto refers to the combination of photography and typography in layout form, specifically in book and advertising formats. Typophoto, for Moholy-Nagy, allowed the designer to communicate clearly and objectively.

UNIVERSAL Herbert Bayer designed this geometric alphabet of lowercase letterforms at the Bauhaus in 1925. This alphabet evokes Bayer's quest to fundamentally rethink letterforms by efficiently stripping them of past values and conventions. Although not mass produced during the first half of the century, it has recently been made into a digital font.

TEXT SOURCES

21 F. T. Marinetti, "The Founding and Manifesto of Futurism," in *F. T. Marinetti: Critical Writings*, ed. Günter Berghaus, trans. Doug Thompson (New York: Farrar, Straus and Giroux, 2006), 11-17. First published in *Le Figaro*, February 20, 1909.

22 Aleksandr Rodchenko, Varvara Stepanova, and Aleksei Gan, "Who We Are: Manifesto of the Constructivist Group," in *Aleksandr Rodchenko: Experiments of the Future*, ed. Alexander N. Lavrentiev (New York: Modern Museum of Art, 2005), 143-145. First published from a typewritten copy c. 1922 preserved in the A. Rodchenko and V. Stepanova archive.

25 El Lissitzky, "Our Book," in *El Lissitzky: Life, Letters, Texts*, ed. Sophie Lissitzky-Küppers, trans. Helene Aldwinckle (London: Thames and Hudson, 1968), 356-359. Abridged from the original version published in *Gutenberg-Jahrbuch* (Mainz, 1926).

33 László Moholy-Nagy, "Typophoto," in *Painting, Photography, Film*, trans. Janet Seligman (Cambridge, MA: MIT Press, 1973), 38-40. First published in German as *Malerei, Photographie, Film* (Munich: Albert Langen Verlag, 1925).

35 Jan Tschichold, "The Principles of the New Typography," in *The New Typography: A Handbook for Modern Designers*, trans. Ruari McLean (Berkeley: University of California Press, 1998), 64-84. First published in German as *Die neue Typographie: Ein Handbuch für Zeitgemäss Schaffende* (Berlin: Bildungs verband der Deutschen Buchdrucker, June 1928).

39 Beatrice Warde, "The Crystal Goblet, or Why Printing Should Be Invisible," in *The Crystal Goblet: Sixteen Essays on Typography* (Cleveland: World Publishing, 1956), 11-17. Originally presented as a speech entitled "Printing Should Be Invisible" to the British Typographers Guild, St. Bride Institute, London, October 7, 1930.

44 Herbert Bayer, "On Typography," *herbert bayer: painter designer architect* (New York: Reinhold, 1967), 75-77.

58 Karl Gerstner, *Designing Programmes* (Zurich: Niggli, 1964), 8-9, 11.

63 Josef Müller-Brockmann, "Grid and Design Philosophy," in *Grid Systems in Graphic Design: A Visual Communication Manual for Graphic Designers, Typographers, and Three Dimensional Designers* (Zurich: Niggli, 1981), 10.

64 Paul Rand, "Good Design Is Goodwill," *AIGA Journal of Graphic Design* 5, no. 3 (1987): 1-2, 14.

70 Robert Venturi, Denise Scott Brown, and Steven Izenour, *Learning from Las Vegas: The Forgotten Symbolism of Architectural Form* (Cambridge, MA: MIT Press, 1972), 3-18.

77 Wolfgang Weingart, *My Way to Typography*, trans. Katherine Wolff and Catherine Schelbert (Baden: Lars Müller, 2000), 268-272, 308-321.

81 Katherine McCoy with David Frej, "Typography as Discourse," *ID Magazine* 35, no. 5 (March-April 1988): 34-37.

84 Lorraine Wild, excerpt from "The Macramé of Resistance," *Emigre* 47 (1998): 14-23. This essay was based on a lecture presented at the 1997 Conference of the American Institute of Graphic Design, New Orleans, November 1998.

87 Paula Scher, "The Dark in the Middle of the Stairs," *Graphis* 264 (November-December 1989): 19.

98 Steven Heller, "The Underground Mainstream," Design Observer blog, April 10, 2008, http://www.designobserver.com/archives/035444.html (accessed June 4, 2008).

102 Jan van Toorn, "Design and Reflexivity," *Visible Language* 28, no. 4 (1994): 316-325.

107 Kalle Lasn, *Design Anarchy* (Vancouver: Adbuster Media, 2006), n.p.

108 Michael Rock, "The Designer as Author," *Eye* 5, no. 20 (Spring 1996): 44-53.

115 Dmitri Siegel, "Designing Our Own Graves," Design Observer blog, June 27, 2006. http://www.designobserver.com/archives/015582.html (accessed April 28, 2008).

119 Jessica Helfand, "Dematerialization of Screen Space," *Screen: Essays on Graphic Design, New Media, and Visual Culture* (New York: Princeton Architectural Press, 2001), 35-39. First published as "Is the Avant-Garde Lost in Space?" *Eye* 9, no. 31 (Spring 1999): 8-9.

124 Kenya Hara, "Computer Technology and Design," and excerpt from "Beyond Modernism," *Designing Design*, trans. Maggie Kinser Hohle and Yukiko Naito (Baden: Lars Müller, 2007), 429-431, 435-436.

127 Lev Manovich, "Import/Export, or Design Workflow and Contemporary Aesthetics," March 2008, http://www.manovich.net (accessed April 28, 2008).

133 Ellen and Julia Lupton, "Univers Strikes Back," 2007. An edited form of this essay was published as "All Together Now," *Print* 61, no. 1 (January-February 2007): 28-30.

BIBLIOGRAPHY

CREATING THE FIELD

Arp, Hans, and El Lissitzky, eds. *The Isms of Art*. Zurich: Eugen Rentsch, 1925.

Ash, Jared, et al. *The Russian Avant-Garde Book, 1910-1934*. New York: Museum of Modern Art, 2002.

Bartram, Alan. *Futurist Typography and the Liberated Text*. New Haven: Yale University Press, 2006.

Bayer, Herbert. "On Typography." In *herbert bayer: painter designer architect*. New York: Reinhold, 1967, 75-77.

Bayer, Herbert, Walter Gropius, and Ise Gropius. *Bauhaus, 1919-1928*. New York: Museum of Modern Art, 1938.

Cohen, Arthur A. *Herbert Bayer: The Complete Work*. Cambridge, MA: MIT Press, 1984.

Dachy, Marc. *The Dada Movement, 1915-1923*. New York: Rizzoli, 1990.

Drucker, Johanna. *The Visible Word: Experimental Typography and Modern Art, 1909-1923*. Chicago: University of Chicago Press, 1994.

Gray, Nicolete. *A History of Lettering: Creative Experiment and Letter Identity*. Oxford: Phaidon Press, 1986.

Heller, Steven. *Merz to Émigré and Beyond: Avant-Garde Magazine Design of the Twentieth Century*. London: Phaidon Press, 2003.

Hultén, Pontus. *Futurism and Futurisms*. New York: Abbeville Press, 1986.

Jaffe, Hans. *De Stijl, 1917-1931: Visions of Utopia*. Minneapolis: Walker Art Center, 1982.

Kostelanetz, Richard, ed. *Moholy-Nagy: An Anthology*. New York: Da Capo Press, 1991.

Lissitzky, El. "Our Book." In *El Lissitzky: Life, Letters, Texts*. Edited by Sophie Lissitzky-Küppers. Translated by Helene Aldwinckle and Mary Whittall. London: Thames and Hudson, 1968, 356-359.

Lissitzky-Küppers, Sophie. *El Lissitzky: Life, Letters, Text*. Translated by Helene Aldwinckle and Mary Whittall. London: Thames and Hudson, 1968.

Lupton, Ellen, and J. Abbott Miller, eds. *The ABC's of Triangle, Square, Circle: The Bauhaus and Design Theory*. New York: Princeton Architectural Press, 2000.

Margolin, Victor. *The Struggle for Utopia: Rodchenko, Lissitzky, Moholy-Nagy, 1917-1946*. Chicago: University of Chicago Press, 1997.

Marinetti, F. T. "The Founding and Manifesto of Futurism." In *Critical Writings: F. T. Marinetti*. Edited by Günter Berghaus. Translated by Doug Thompson. New York: Farrar, Straus and Giroux, 2006, 11-17.

McLean, Ruari. *Jan Tschichold: Typographer*. Boston: D.R. Godine, 1975.

Moholy-Nagy, László. "Typophoto." In *Painting, Photography, Film*. Translated by Janet Seligman. Cambridge: MIT Press, 1973, 38-40.

Passuth, Krisztina. *Moholy-Nagy*. London: Thames and Hudson, 1987.

Richter, Hans. *Dada: Art and Anti-Art*. London: Thames and Hudson, 1966.

Rodchenko, Aleksandr. "Who We Are: Manifesto of the Constructivist Group." *Aleksandr Rodchenko: Experiments for the Future*. Edited by Alexander N. Lavrentiev. New York: Museum of Modern Art, 2005, 143-145.

Rowell, Margit and Deborah Wye. *The Russian Avant-Garde Book: 1910-1934*. New York: Museum of Modern Art, 2002.

Spencer, Herbert. *Pioneers of Modern Typography*. London: Lund Humphries, 1969.

Tschichold, Jan. "The Principles of the New Typography." In *The New Typography: A Handbook for Modern Designers*. Translated by Ruari McLean. Berkeley: University of California Press, 1998, 64-84.

Tschichold, Jan. *Asymmetric Typography*. Translated by Ruari McLean. New York: Reinhold, 1967.

Tschichold, Jan. *The Form of the Book: Essays on the Morality of Good Design*. Translated by Hajo Hadeler. Point Roberts, WA: Hartley & Marks, 1991.

Van Doesburg, Theo, Hans M. Wingler, and H. L. C. Jaffé. *Principles of Neo-Plastic Art*. Translated by Janet Seligman. Greenwich, CT: New York Graphic Society, 1968.

Warde, Beatrice. "The Crystal Goblet, or Why Printing Should Be Invisible." In *The Crystal Goblet: Sixteen Essays on Typography*. Cleveland: World Publishing, 1956, 11-17.

BUILDING ON SUCCESS

Benjamin, Walter. *Reflections: Essays, Aphorisms, Autobiographical Writings*. Edited by Peter Demetz. Translated by Edmund Jephcott. New York: Harcourt Brace Jovanovich, 1978.

Blackwell, Lewis, and David Carson. "Conversation." In *The End of Print: The Graphic Design of David Carson*. London: Laurence King, 1995, 27-29.

DeKoven, Marianne. *Utopia Limited: The Sixties and the Emergence of the Postmodern*. Durham: Duke University Press, 2004.

Gerstner, Karl. *Designing Programmes*. Zurich: Niggli, 1968.

Gerstner, Karl. *Review of 5 x 10 Years of Graphic Design etc.* Ostfildern-Ruit, Germany: Hatje Cantz, 2001.

Greiman, April. *Hybrid Imagery: The Fusion of Technology of Graphic Design*. New York: Watson-Guptill, 1990.

Heller, Steven. *Paul Rand*. London: Phaidon Press, 1999.

Hollis, Richard. *Swiss Graphic Design: The Origins and Growth of an International Style, 1920-1965*. London: Laurence King, 2006.

Lupton, Ellen, and J. Abbott Miller. *Design Writing Research: Writing on Graphic Design*. New York: Kiosk, 1996.

Marchand, Roland. *Creating the Corporate Soul: The Rise of Public Relations and Corporate Imagery in American Big Business*. Berkeley: University of California Press, 2001.

Marcuse, Herbert. *One-Dimensional Man: Studies in the Ideology of Advanced Industrial Society*. Boston: Beacon Press, 1991.

McCoy, Katherine with David Frej. "Typography as Discourse." *ID* 35, no. 5 (March-April 1988): 34-37.

McCoy, Katherine, and Michael McCoy. *Cranbrook Design: The New Discourse*. New York: Rizzoli, 1990.

McLuhan, Marshall. *The Gutenberg Galaxy: The Making of Typographic Man*. Toronto: University of Toronto Press, 1966.

Müller, Lars, ed. *Josef Müller-Brockmann*. Baden: Lars Müller, 1994.

Müller-Brockmann, Josef. *The Graphic Designer and His Design Problems*. New York: Hastings House, 1983.

Müller-Brockmann, Josef. "Grid and Design Philosophy." In *Grid Systems in Graphic Design: A Visual Communication Manual for Graphic Designers, Typographers, and Three-Dimensional Designers.* 10. Niederteufen, Switzerland: Niggli, 1981.

Poynor, Rick. *No More Rules: Graphic Design and Postmodernism.* New Haven: Yale University Press, 2003.

Purcell, Kerry William. *Josef Müller-Brockmann.* New York: Phaidon Press, 2006.

Rand, Paul. *Design, Form, and Chaos.* New Haven: Yale University Press, 1993.

Rand, Paul. "Good Design Is Goodwill." *AIGA Journal of Graphic Design* 5, no. 3 (1987): 1-2, 14.

Rand, Paul. *Thoughts on Design.* London: Studio Vista, 1970.

Scher, Paula. *Make It Bigger.* New York: Princeton Architectural Press, 2002.

Venturi, Robert, Denise Scott Brown, and Steven Izenour. *Learning from Las Vegas: The Forgotten Symbolism of Architectural Form.* Cambridge, MA: MIT Press, 1972.

Weingart, Wolfgang. "Fourth Independent Project: Letters and Typographic Elements in New Context" and "Fifth Independent Project: Typography as Endless Repetition." In *My Way to Typography.* Translated by Katherine Wolff and Catherine Schelbert. Baden: Lars Müller, 2000, 268-272 and 308-321.

Wild, Lorraine. "The Macrame of Resistance." *Emigre* 47 (Summer 1998): 14-23.

MAPPING THE FUTURE

Abrams, Janet, and Peter Hall, eds. *Else/Where: Mapping New Cartographies of Networks and Territories.* Minneapolis: University of Minnesota Design Institute, 2006.

Bennett, Audrey, ed. *Design Studies: Theory and Research in Graphic Design.* New York: Princeton Architectural Press, 2006.

Bierut, Michael, William Drenttel, and Steven Heller, eds. *Looking Closer 5: Critical Writings on Graphic Design.* New York: Allsworth Press, 2007.

Fiell, Charlotte, and Peter Fiell, eds. *Graphic Design for the 21st Century: 100 of the World's Best Designers.* Cologne: Taschen, 2003.

Galloway, Alexander R., and Eugene Thacker. *The Exploit: A Theory of Networks.* Minneapolis: University of Minneapolis Press, 2007.

Hara, Kenya. *Designing Design.* Translated by Maggie Kinser Hohle and Yukiko Naito. Baden: Lars Müller, 2007.

Helfand, Jessica, and John Maeda. "Dematerialization of Screen Space." In *Screen: Essays on Graphic Design, New Media, and Visual Culture.* New York: Princeton Architectural Press, 2001, 35-39.

Heller, Steven. "Underground Mainstream." Design Observer blog, April 10, 2008. http://www.designobserver.com/archives/035444.html (accessed June 4, 2008).

Heller, Steven, and Veronique Vienne, eds. *Citizen Designer: Perspectives on Design Responsibility.* New York: Allsworth Press, 2003.

Ilyin, Natalia. *Chasing the Perfect: Thoughts on Modernist Design in Our Time.* New York: Metropolis, 2006.

Klein, Naomi. *No Logo.* New York: Picador, 2002.

Lasn, Kalle. *Design Anarchy.* Vancouver: Adbuster Media, 2006.

Lasn, Kalle. *Culture Jam: The Uncooling of America.* New York: Eagle Brook, 1999.

Laurel, Brenda. *Utopian Entrepreneur.* Cambridge, MA: MIT Press, 2001.

Manovich, Lev. "Import/Export, or Design Workflow and Contemporary Aesthetics." March 2008, http://www.manovich.net (accessed April 28, 2008).

Manovich, Lev. *The Language of New Media.* Cambridge, MA: MIT Press, 2002.

Lévy, Pierre. *Cyberculture.* Translated by Robert Bononno. Minneapolis: University of Minneapolis Press, 2001.

Lovink, Geert. *Zero Comments: Blogging and Critical Internet Culture.* New York: Routledge, 2008.

Lupton, Ellen and Julia. "All Together Now," *Print* 61, no. 1 (January-February 2007): 28-30.

Maeda, John. *The Laws of Simplicity: Design, Technology, Business, Life.* Cambridge, MA: MIT Press, 2006.

Poynor, Rick. "First Things First Manifesto 2000," *AIGA Journal of Graphic Design* 17, no. 2 (1999): 6-7.

Poynor, Rick. *Jan van Toorn: Critical Practice.* Rotterdam: 010 Publishers, 2008.

Rock, Michael. "The Designer as Author." *Eye* 5, no. 20 (Spring 1996): 44-53.

Siegel, Dmitri. "Designing Our Own Graves." Design Observer blog, June 27, 2006. http://www.designobserver.com (accessed April 28, 2008).

Toorn, Jan van. "Design and Reflexivity." *Visible Language* 28, no. 4 (1994): 316-325.

Toorn, Jan van. *Design's Delight: Method and Means of a Dialogic Approach.* Rotterdam: 010 Publishers, 2006.

GENERAL HISTORY|THEORY

Adams, Hazard, and Leroy Searle, eds. *Critical Theory since 1965.* Tallahassee: Florida State University Press, 1986.

Barthes, Roland. *Image/Music/Text.* Translated by Stephen Heath. New York: Hill and Wang, 1977.

Baudrillard, Jean. *For a Critique of the Political Economy of the Sign.* Translated by Charles Levin. St. Louis: Telos Press, 1981.

Bourdieu, Pierre. *Language and Symbolic Power.* Cambridge, MA: Harvard University Press, 1991.

Derrida, Jacques. *Of Grammatology.* Translated by Gayatri Chakravorty Spivak. Baltimore: Johns Hopkins University Press, 1976.

Drucker, Johanna, and Emily McVarish. *Graphic Design History: A Critical Guide.* Upper Saddle River, NJ: Prentice Hall, 2008.

Eskilson, Stephen J. *Graphic Design: A New History.* New Haven: Yale University Press, 2007.

Foucault, Michel. "What Is an Author?" In Josué Harari, ed. *Textual Strategies: Perspectives in Post-Structuralist Criticism.* Ithaca: Cornell University Press, 1979, 142-160.

Hollis, Richard. *Graphic Design: A Concise History* (World of Art). London: Thames and Hudson, 1994.

Jubert, Roxane. *Typography and Graphic Design: From Antiquity to the Present.* Translated by Deke Dusinberre and David Radzinowicz. Paris: Flammarion, 2006.

Meggs, Philip B. *A History of Graphic Design.* New York: John Wiley and Sons, 1998.

Millman, Debbie. *How to Think Like a Great Graphic Designer.* New York: Allsworth Press, 2007.

Tyson, Lois. *Critical Theory Today: A User-Friendly Guide.* New York: Routledge, 2006.

IMAGE CREDITS

Inside front, inside back illustration by Eduard Kachan

18, 49, 54, 55, 93 Herbert Bayer, reprinted courtesy of Jonathon Bayer.

20, 50, 51 F. T. Marinetti, courtesy The Beinecke Rare Book and Manuscript Library © 2008 Artists Rights Society (ARS), New York / SIAE, Rome.

23, 52 Aleksandr Rodchenko © Estate of Aleksandr Rodchenko/RAO, Moscow/VAGA, New York, New York.

31, 53 El Lissitzky, courtesy Slavic and Baltic Division, The New York Public Library, Astor, Lenox and Tilden Foundations, © 2008 Artists Rights Society (ARS), New York / VG Bild-Kunst, Bonn.

32 László Moholy-Nagy, photography Dan Meyers © 2008 Artists Rights Society (ARS), New York / VG Bild-Kunst, Bonn.

36, 37, 38, 55 Jan Tschichold, © University of California Press, by permission of University of California Press.

43 Beatrice Warde photo, courtesy of Dr. Shelley Gruendler and the St. Bride Library, London.

56, 91 Josef Müller-Brockmann © 2008 Artists Rights Society (ARS), New York / Pro Litteris, Zurich.

62 Josef Müller-Brockmann © 1981 Verlag Niggli AG.

66, 69, 92 Paul Rand, reprinted courtesy Marion Rand.

72 Robert Venturi, Denise Scott Brown, and Steven Izenour, © 1977 Massachusetts Institute of Technology, by permission of The MIT Press.

137B Ellen Lupton, *Graphic Design: The New Basics* (New York: Princeton Architectural Press, 2008). Photography included within spread, clockwise from top right, Jason Okutake, Jeremy Botts, and Kelley McIntyre.

137T Ellen Lupton and J. Abbott Miller, *Design Writing Research: Writing on Graphic Design* (New York: Kiosk, 1996).

TEXT CREDITS

21 F. T. Marinetti, "The Founding and Manifesto of Futurism," © 2007 Artists Rights Society (ARS), New York / SAIE, Rome.

22 Aleksandr Rodchenko, "Who We Are: Manifesto of the Constructivist Group," © Estate of Aleksandr Rodchenko / RAO, Moscow / VAGA, New York, New York.

25 El Lissitzky, "Our Book," in *El Lissitzky: Life, Letters, Text,* ed. Sophie Lissitzky-Küppers, trans. Helene Aldwinckle and Mary Whittall. Reprinted by permission of Thames and Hudson, Ltd., London.

32 László Moholy-Nagy, *Painting, Photography, Film,* 38–40, © 1969 Lund Humphries, by permission of The MIT Press.

35 Jan Tschichold, "The Principles of the New Typography," in *The New Typography: A Handbook for Modern Designers,* © University of California Press, by permission of University of California Press.

44 Herbert Bayer, "On Typography," reprinted courtesy of Jonathon Bayer.

63 Josef Müller-Brockmann, "Grid and Design Philosophy," *Grid Systems in Graphic Design* 10, © 1981 Verlag Niggli AG.

64 Paul Rand, "Good Design Is Goodwill," reprinted courtesy of AIGA.

70 Robert Venturi, Denise Scott Brown, and Steven Izenour, *Learning from Las Vegas, revised edition: The Forgotten Symbolism of Architectural Form,* text from pages 3–18, © 1977 Massachusetts Institute of Technology, by permission of The MIT Press.

Special thanks to Karl Gerstner, Kenya Hara, Jessica Helfand, Steven Heller, Kalle Lasn, Ellen and Julia Lupton, Katherine McCoy, Lev Manovich, Michael Rock, Paula Scher, Dmitri Siegel, Jan van Toorn, Wolfgang Weingart, and Lorraine Wild for permission to reproduce their work.

INDEX

COLOPHON

BOOK DESIGNER: Helen Armstrong

EDITOR: Clare Jacobson, Princeton Architectural Press

TYPOGRAPHY: Interstate designed by Tobias Frere-Jones, 1993;
Seria designed by Martin Majoor, 2000.

ABOUT THE AUTHOR

Helen Armstrong is a graphic designer and educator based in
Baltimore, Maryland. She has taught and lectured at the University
of Mississippi, University of Tennessee, University of Maryland, and
Maryland Institute College of Art (where she teaches graphic design
theory to seniors and graduate students). She has an MA in English
literature, an MA in Publications Design, and an MFA in graphic
design. In addition to teaching, Armstrong also works as principal and
creative director of her company, Strong Design. Her design work—for
such clients as Sage College of Albany, USInternetworking, and New
College of Florida—has won regional and international awards. Her work
has been included in numerous publications in the United States and
the United Kingdom, including *HOW International Design Annual, The
Complete Typographer,* and *The Typography Workbook.*